INTERVENTION

	DATE DUE		
JUL 0 9 1997			
AUG 1 9 1997			
SEP 0 4 1997			
DEC 2 2 1997			
FEB 23 '06			
JA 1 1 '10			
FE 0 1 '10			
A 1 9 2018			

INTERVENTION

How to help someone who doesn't want help

A step-by-step guide for families and friends of chemically dependent persons

by VERNON E. JOHNSON

Johnson Institute Books
Minneapolis

Johnson Institute, 7205 Ohms Lane
Minneapolis, Minnesota 55439-2159

Library of Congress Cataloging in Publication Data

Johnson, Vernon E.
  Intervention, how to help someone who doesn't want
help.

  Includes index.
    1. Alcoholics—Rehabilitation. 2. Alcoholics—Family
relationships. 3. Drug abuse—Treatment.
  I. Title
  HV5278.J64 1986   362.2'9   86-7449
  ISBN: 0-935908-31-5

PRINTED IN THE UNITED STATES OF AMERICA

10   9   8

97— $8.95

From former First Lady Betty Ford
to Vernon Johnson, January, 1986:

Dear Vern,

Congratulations on the 20th anniversary of the Johnson Institute. Over that 20 year period, you have certainly been a pioneer in the changes that have occurred in the treatment and awareness of alcohol and drug dependency.

As one of the people who has benefited from your intervention process, I offer you a hearty thanks — from all the members of the Ford family.

The past seven and a half years of my life have led me on an incredible path. You provided the possibility for the first step. I treasure each time that my path crosses with yours.

With warm best wishes,

Betty Ford

These pages are gratefully dedicated
to Burns and Tippy Hoffman,
who from the outset deemed ignorance
to be the chief enemy and whose friendship
has been a constant encouragement.

ACKNOWLEDGMENTS

In the early 1960s, intervention was a theory which seemed to fly in the face of long-established opinion and practice which held that nothing could be done with alcoholics until they "hit bottom" or that only those chemically dependent people who were "properly motivated" would respond positively to professionally delivered remedial care.

Scarcely more than two decades later, the process of intervention described in the following pages has gained such widespread acceptance as to be practiced at virtually every economic and social level in the United States. To attempt to acknowledge those responsible for bringing about so rapid and thoroughgoing a change in a basic approach to this deadly epidemic in our midst is obviously an impossible task. They are too many by now even to list. One also hesitates to be specific in an effort to illustrate how varied and influential so many of these groups offering intervention processes to their stricken members are, since to name some is to leave unnamed many others equally committed and caring. However, among those who have come to us for training at the Institute over the past 20 years have been representatives of both corporate management and organized labor as Employee Assistance Programs sprang into being. They have come to us from the several branches of our country's armed services with notable programs of intervention and treatment developing particularly in the U.S. Navy and the U.S.

Air Force. State medical associations have developed programs of intervention with impaired physicians. Lawyers began helping lawyers. Church denominations became increasingly involved, as in the Episcopal church, where every diocese is now charged with having an active commission on chemical dependency and intervention training. The list goes on and on, and I am deeply grateful to them all. However, a very special thanks must go to the Airline Pilots Association and their medical office under the caring leadership of Dr. Richard Masters; the Cargill Company, where one of the very first Employee Assistance Programs was organized; and the Rutgers Summer School of Alcohol Studies, where so many students were exposed to this training for the first time.

I express my gratitude to the board of the Johnson Institute itself. Obviously without their first and primary commitment to the educational task of our staff, none of this would have happened. Finally and particularly, I am grateful to Pamela Espeland, whose editorial skills are discernible throughout the pages that follow.

CONTENTS

PART II: INTERVENING WITH CHEMICAL DEPENDENCY

INTRODUCTION

You are reading this book because you suspect that someone you care about is chemically dependent. That someone may be a spouse or a child, a parent or a cousin, a coworker or a neighbor or a friend. The drug of choice may be alcohol, marijuana, cocaine, amphetamines ("uppers"), barbiturates ("downers"), or some combination of these. What it is does not matter; what matters is that the person is abusing or misusing it, and that this is causing problems for him or her *and for you.*

These problems may range all the way from mildly erratic behaviors on the individual's part to major personality changes and physical deterioration. Maybe the individual is performing poorly at work. Maybe there's been one or more DWIs (driving while intoxicated) or DUIs (driving under the influence). Maybe things are tense around the house (or office). Maybe you have caught the person telling lies, breaking promises, or making excuses that are directly related to using. Maybe there have been occasions when the person has been hospitalized, or taken to detox, or jailed. Or maybe you simply have the uneasy feeling that something is wrong somewhere, and chemical dependency could be the cause.

Fortunately for that person, *you want to help.* At the moment, though, you are not sure how to go about it. Furthermore, the person does not seem willing to accept help from you or anyone else. In fact, he or she may loudly deny that a problem exists, or even blame it on you!

If you are like most people, you may believe that there is nothing you can do except wait for the person to "hit bottom" and then try to pick up the pieces. For the past 20 years, our task at the Johnson Institute has been to prove that just the opposite is true. Waiting is too dangerous. It is also cruel. It allows an already bad situation to get worse. If a friend wanted to jump off a bridge, would you let him do it before you reached out a hand to stop him? Of course not; and neither must you stand by and watch the chemically dependent person plumb the depths of suffering and despair before doing something about it. You don't have to bide your time until your family breaks up, or the person is fired from his or her job — or kills someone in a car accident. You can reach out *now*.

You may also believe that only the experts — physicians, psychiatrists, chemical dependency counselors — are equipped and able to help the chemically dependent person. That is not necessarily the case. Another thing we have learned at the Johnson Institute is that *anyone who sincerely wants to help, can help.* You do not need a clinical background or special expertise. You should, however, have some understanding of what chemical dependency is and how it affects its victims, and this is the focus of Part I of this book, "Learning About Chemical Dependency." With this information in hand, you may then decide whether to seek help from one of the many capable professionals with experience in this field.

The important thing is to *take action* — and soon. By definition, a chemically dependent person is out of touch with reality. Through a process called *intervention*, you can play an important role in moving the person you care about back toward reality, recovery, and a richer, fuller, longer life. Thousands of concerned people like you have done it for their relatives and friends; thousands of chemically dependent persons are alive and well today as proof that it works. Part II of this book, "Intervening With Chemical Dependency," describes this process and the steps involved in preparing for it, initiating it, and seeing it through.

You have already taken the first step by reading this far. While subsequent steps may not be quite as easy, they are just as achievable.

They are also essential. Because the bottom line is this: *Unless the chemically dependent person gets help, he or she will die prematurely.* Chemical dependency is a disease that kills. It is also a disease from which people can and do recover.

You can make sure that the person you know is one who does recover.

PART I

LEARNING ABOUT
CHEMICAL DEPENDENCY

▶ Chapter 1 ◀

THE DISEASE OF CHEMICAL DEPENDENCY

Perhaps you are unaware that chemical dependency is a disease. But it is — just like diabetes or the mumps.

It is vital that you both understand and accept this concept. Once you do, you can begin to realize that the person who abuses or misuses alcohol or drugs is not doing it deliberately, but because he or she is sick. Some of your confusion, frustration, and anger will subside, and you will be able to approach the situation more objectively and constructively.

You would not blame your child for coming down with the flu. Instead, you would take your child to the doctor, have the disease properly diagnosed, and do whatever you could to speed your child on the way to recovery. Similarly, *you cannot blame the chemically dependent person for being chemically dependent.* What you *can* do is help him or her to get the care that is needed.

If you are finding the disease concept difficult to grasp, you are not alone. Some physicians still do not accept it. Some even prescribe drugs to alleviate the symptoms of chemical dependency, leading to new dependencies.

It was not until 1956 that the American Medical Association formally recognized alcoholism as a disease. Until then, most medical and psychiatric professionals believed that it was a symptom of some other underlying emotional or psychological disorder. As a result, the usual approach went something like this: "Let's find out what's *really* wrong with you. If we can get at that and correct it, then you will no longer have the need to drink." It was thought that the drinking problem would take care of itself — disappear spontaneously — if that other disorder could be discovered and addressed. Months, and sometimes years, were spent in treatment that did not work. Meanwhile the sick person's condition steadily worsened.

Once alcoholism* was identified as a disease, it became possible to learn more about it.

---

* When we use the term "alcoholism" in this book, we are referring to all other types of chemical dependency as well. The symptoms of dependency are essentially the same, and the need for intervention is just as urgent whether the person is abusing diet pills, marijuana, cocaine, hallucinogens, amphetamines, barbiturates, tranquilizers, or whatever.

The process of intervention translates across the board and across age groups. There has been a tendency in some treatment circles to approach drugs idiosyncratically when it is far more useful to approach them generically. At the Johnson Institute, we do not distinguish between the alcoholic who drinks only beer and the alcoholic who drinks only gin; similarly, we do not distinguish between the drug user who smokes marijuana and the drug user who mainlines heroin. And, by extension, we do not treat the drug user any differently from the alcoholic. *All* are caught up in the emotional syndrome we will describe later; *all* need help; *all* can benefit greatly from intervention.

There is also a widespread belief that young people can't get into the same sort of trouble with chemical dependency as adults. This is simply not true. Nobody is "too young" to develop a harmful and eventually fatal dependency on alcohol or drugs. And nobody is "too old" to recover.

What We Know About The Disease

1. The disease can be described.

A disease is a condition which is describable across a population. If your daughter wakes up one morning with red spots all over her body, and you take her to the doctor, the doctor will take one look at those red spots and (provided they're a certain kind of red spots) will correctly diagnose a case of measles. Not because the doctor knows anything about your child's personality, or habits, or friends, but because measles are measles regardless of who gets them.

We are now able to diagnose chemical dependency in much the same way. A symptomatology — a list of distinct characteristics of the disease — is available, enabling us to recognize its presence and effects.

One of the symptoms of alcoholism is the compulsion to drink. This compulsion is evident in drinking that is *inappropriate, unpredictable, excessive, and constant.*

The alcoholic's behavior fluctuates between extremes that confuse and bewilder the people around him or her. He or she may be unaware of the compulsion, but it is always there. When confronted with it, he or she might say, "Compulsion? What compulsion? A compulsion means that you *have* to have a drink. But I'm not like that! I always *decide* whether or not I'm going to drink, so I can't possibly be an alcoholic."

To the person close to the alcoholic, that may even sound reasonable. To an objective outside observer, however, it becomes obvious that sooner or later the "decision" is always the same: to drink. Or, in the case of the drug addict, to use.

2. The disease is primary.

Rather than being a symptom of an underlying emotional or physical disorder, chemical dependency *causes* many such problems or aggravates those that already exist. And these cannot be treated effectively unless the chemical dependency is treated *first*.

It is estimated that alcohol is involved in anywhere from 25 to 50 percent of all admissions to hospitals and mental hospitals. Gastritis, cirrhosis of the liver, the deterioration of blood vessels in the brain, the breakdown of the lining of the esophagus, alcoholic myopathy (a generalized weakness in the muscles), impotence in men and menstrual difficulties in women, mental deterioration, and alcohol-related heart disease, among others, continue to escalate for as long as the sick person keeps drinking. Social problems and family problems keep getting worse.

Chemical dependency seems to rest on a human life in such a way that it effectively blocks any other care we might want to deliver to whatever else is wrong with the individual. For example, if an alcoholic has a diseased liver, not even the best practitioner can deliver lasting care to that individual through the alcoholism. That must be lifted off first, to clear the way for healing.

The same is true for emotional problems. Not even the best psychiatric care can have any lasting effects until the drinking or using stops. That must happen before recovery can begin.

3. *The disease follows a predictable and progressive course.*
The doctor who diagnoses your daughter's measles is able to say, "Sorry, but for the next several days some or all of these things are going to happen, because that's the way measles are." The disease runs a predictable course.

So does chemical dependency. Unlike many other diseases, however, chemical dependency is also *progressive*. This means that it *always* gets worse if left untreated.

There may be plateaus when the drinking or using behavior seems to remain constant for months or even years, and occasionally some event will trigger what appears to be a "spontaneous" improvement. But the disease moves inexorably toward greater and more serious deterioration over time unless it is arrested. And because it is a *multiphasic* disease, it affects the individual on all planes — physical, mental, emotional, and spiritual.

4. *The disease is permanent, or chronic.*

Here is where we begin to see how truly serious the disease of chemical dependency is. Nobody has the measles over a lifetime, but once a person becomes chemically dependent, he or she remains so forever.

It used to be believed that chemical dependency was "learned" and could therefore be "unlearned." Now we know that this is not so. It is contracted, like any other disease, and it never goes away.

Fortunately it *can* be arrested, and dependent persons can go on to live happy, healthy, productive lives — *as long as they abstain from mood-altering chemicals.* Relapse — the return to drinking or using — is an ever-present danger; this is another side to the chronicity of the disease.

There are countless tales of alcoholic or drug dependent men and women who have remained abstinent for many years and then returned to drinking or using in attempted moderation. Only rare exceptions have been successful; the rest have soon found themselves drinking or using even more heavily and self-destructively than before. There are stories of alcoholics who have stayed dry and then begun regular use of tranquilizers under a physician's orders. Before long, they have become addicted to the prescribed drug, and have also started drinking again.

Some treatment programs purport to teach the alcoholic "how to drink" or the addict "how to use." Our experience is in direct contradiction to this, with the exceptions being very few and far between.

In other words, the safest and most responsible alternative for the chemically dependent person who wants to recover is total abstinence from *all* mood-altering drugs — alcohol, amphetamines, barbiturates, minor tranquilizers, even cough syrups containing codeine. A single slip can precipitate a return to the active stages of the disease.

With treatment, such abstinence does not have to be bleak and miserable. Instead, it becomes life-affirming, even joyful. There's a saying among Alcoholics Anonymous (A.A.) members: "The best day drinking is not as good as the hardest day sober."

5. *The disease is fatal.*

A person whose chemical dependency is not arrested will eventually die from it, and die prematurely. Left unchecked, *chemical dependency is a 100 percent fatal disease*. We are not talking about a bad habit; we are talking about a life-or-death situation!

Insurance company statistics indicate that an alcoholic who continues to drink has an average life span 12 years shorter than the nonalcoholic in our society. The stated cause of premature death may be *physical* (heart disease, liver ailments, bleeding ulcers), *accidental* (car crashes, on-the-job accidents), or *emotional* (depression-related suicide).

Death certificates use a lot of euphemisms for chemical dependency, but the result is still the same: the victim is dead, with alcohol or drugs the causative agent.

6. *The disease is treatable.*

Primary, predictable, chronic, and fatal: these four characteristics make it seem as if chemical dependency is the worst disease around. It would be, were it not for one more very important characteristic: *it can be treated and arrested*. And, in fact, it has a predictable response to a specific form of care. The proof is found in the millions of people who are recovering today. Of the referrals we make to treatment, *seven or eight out of every ten emerge successful.*

Chemical dependency cannot be cured, which is why persons who have stopped drinking or using, gone through treatment, and set about fully living again are described as recover*ing*, not recovered. Recovery is a process and a lifelong commitment.

⇨✕⇦

One thing we do not yet know is how the disease of chemical dependency gets its start. Various theories have been proposed, although none has yet been proved.

Some suggest that it may be hereditary; it does tend to run in families, and there is about a 25 percent chance that the child of one or more alcoholic parents will become alcoholic. But that does not explain why the other 75 percent will not, or why many alcoholics come from families where chemical dependency has not (apparently) been a problem in the past. Other theories claim that chemical dependency is related to a specific personality type. But there are millions of alcoholics who do not fit any particular profile.

What is clear is that all sorts of people become chemically dependent, some for no apparent reason. On the other hand, it seems that some people cannot become chemically dependent no matter how hard they try!

We *do* know that chemical dependency is not caused by a lack of willpower, or weakness of character, or some flaw in a person's moral structure. It is not a form of mental illness. Nor is it the result of external influences — an unhappy marriage, trouble on the job, peer pressure. This means, of course, that if someone you care about is alcoholic or drug dependent, *it is not your fault.**

We also know that approximately 10 percent of the drinkers in America today will become alcoholic at some point during their lives. Currently an estimated 10-20 million people are sick with the disease. The good news is that recovery is possible for them.

How To Tell If Someone You Know Is Chemically Dependent

Now that you know the characteristics of the disease, how can you go about determining whether someone you care about is suffering from it? Needless to say, this is not something that should be taken lightly. Suspecting that someone is chemically dependent, and saying so to the person's face, are two very different matters!

Some people believe that you cannot label another person an alcoholic; that this must come from the person himself or herself. But as we shall see, the chemically dependent person is often the last to recognize (or admit) that he or she has a problem. So it may, in fact, be up to you to observe the signs and draw the conclusions.

The following test, while not a diagnostic tool, can help you to determine if your suspicions are founded. Answer each question with a "yes" or a "no."

---

* If you learn only *one* thing from this book, let it be this. *You are not responsible* for the disease of chemical dependency that has taken hold in the person you care about. You may be feeling guilty anyway; we will talk in more detail later about the reasons for those feelings. For now, however, try to believe — or at least consider! — that nothing you have ever done could have resulted in that person's illness.

1. Is the person drinking (or using any other drug) more now than he or she did in the past?

2. Are you ever afraid to be around the person when he or she is drinking or using drugs — because of the possibility of verbal or physical abuse?

3. Has the person ever forgotten or denied things that happened during a drinking or using episode?

4. Do you worry about the person's drinking or drug use?

5. Does the person refuse to talk about his or her drinking or drug use — or even to discuss the possibility that he or she might have a problem with it?

6. Has the person broken promises to control or stop his or her drinking or drug use?

7. Has the person ever lied about his or her drinking or using, or tried to hide it from you?

8. Have you ever been embarrassed by the person's drinking or drug use?

9. Have you ever lied to anyone else about the person's drinking or drug use?

10. Have you ever made excuses for the way the person behaved while drinking or using?

11. Are most of the person's friends heavy drinkers or drug users?

12. Does the person make excuses for, or try to justify, his or her drinking or using?

13. Do you feel guilty about the person's drinking or drug use?

14. Are holidays and social functions unpleasant for you because of the person's drinking or drug use?

15. Do you feel anxious or tense around the person because of his or her drinking or drug use?

16. Have you ever helped the person to "cover up" for a drinking or using episode — by calling his or her employer, or telling others that he or she is feeling "sick"?

17. Does the person deny that he or she has a drinking problem because he or she only drinks beer (or wine)? Or deny that he or she has a drug problem because use is "limited" to marijuana, or diet pills, or some other supposedly "harmless" substance?

18. Does the person's behavior change noticeably when he or she is drinking or using? (For example: a normally quiet person might become loud and talkative, or a normally mild-mannered person might become quick to anger.)

19. Does the person avoid social functions where alcohol will not be served, or drugs will not be available or permitted?

20. Does the person insist on going only to restaurants that serve alcohol?

21. To your knowledge, has the person ever driven a car while intoxicated or under the influence of drugs?

22. Has the person ever received a DWI or DUI?

23. Are you afraid to ride with the person after he or she has been drinking or using?

24. Has anyone else talked to you about the person's drinking or using behavior?

25. Has the person ever expressed remorse for his or her behavior during a drinking or using episode?

26. If you are married to the person and have children, are the children afraid of the person while he or she is drinking or using?

27. Does the person seem to have a low self-image?

28. Have you ever found alcohol or drugs that the person has hidden?

29. Is the person having financial difficulties that seem to be related to his or her drinking or drug use?

30. Does the person look forward to times when he or she can drink or use drugs?

If you answered "yes" to any three of these questions, then there is a good chance that the person you care about has a drinking or drug problem. If you answered "yes" to any five, then the chance is even greater. And if you answered "yes" to seven or more, you can feel safe in assuming that the person definitely has a problem with chemical dependency.

There is a very simple definition of chemical dependency that you may find helpful:

If the use of alcohol or other drugs is causing *any* continuing disruption in an individual's personal, social, spiritual or economic life, and the individual *does not stop using*, he or she is chemically dependent.

The refusal to stop using — even when using is clearly having an impact on the individual's life — signals a pathological attachment to the chemical and is one of the surest signs of harmful dependency.

The *non*-chemically dependent person might have *one* brush with the law. He or she might have *one* reprimand from his or her employer. He or she might have family problems over *one* drinking or using episode. But that *one* event will be sufficient to make him or her think, "If I'm going to have that kind of trouble, I'm going to cut this stuff out!" And he or she will.

The chemically dependent person, on the other hand, will keep using the drug even though it causes continuing problems in any or all of the relationships that are important to him or her. By these actions, he or she is saying, "Family, friends, and job are important to me, but drinking or using is *more* important." This is attaching an emotional importance to an inert substance — an obviously abnormal response, and one that indicates the presence of the disease of chemical dependency.

▶ Chapter 2 ◀

THE EMOTIONAL SYNDROME
OF CHEMICAL DEPENDENCY

If you have come closer to recognizing chemical dependency as a disease, you have taken a giant step toward helping the person about whom you are concerned. You should now know that he or she will probably be one of the *last* people to come to that awareness.

Slow acceptance (or no acceptance) of the problem is another symptom of the illness. The reasons for this denial are found in the ways that chemical dependency affects the individual and the people around him or her, and in the attitudes of our drinking and using culture — which actually serve to *compound* and strengthen the denial.

Alcohol is our most common and widely used social drug.* It is both socially and legally sanctioned; anyone of age can buy it and use it. It is routinely served in public restaurants and private

---

* Cocaine and marijuana are being used by more people than ever before — and at ever younger ages. A recent survey indicates that within the next two years, more than one out of every five high school students will have tried cocaine.

homes, at baseball games and office parties (although this is happening somewhat less frequently these days), at theaters and on airplanes. The popping of champagne corks is required at our celebrations; no dinner is complete without wine; and we even allow our children to take their first sips of beer while sitting on our laps.

At the Johnson Institute, we have seen enough evidence to arrive at the sad conclusion that anyone in our culture who *can* become chemically dependent, *will* become chemically dependent. But it is not only Americans who are prone to this disease; the dilemma is worldwide. The Soviet Union has a serious alcohol problem that it has only recently acknowledged publicly. There are millions of alcoholics in France, in England, in Italy, in Spain, in China, in Central and South America — anywhere, in fact, where the consumption of alcohol is not expressly forbidden by a national religion. (And even in countries where it is, use is increasing.)

The extent of the problem — and the fact that it cuts across all racial, social, economic, and geographic barriers — is further proof that chemical dependency is indeed a disease. Why would so many millions of people choose a behavior that is clearly self-destructive? How could it be possible for people everywhere on the face of the planet to develop the *same* symptoms, the *same* compulsions, the *same* related disorders, if what they really suffer from is the lack of self-control?

Most people, when they come down with a disease, will set about trying to find treatment for it, provided that medical help is available to them. Here is where chemical dependency distinguishes itself as a disease unlike any other. *The people who have it generally do not seek treatment of their own volition because they are not aware that they have it.* This is because chemical dependency is universally accompanied by an *emotional syndrome* that is unique to it and effectively blocks the consciousness that it exists.

What We Know About
the Emotional Syndrome

To understand this emotional syndrome, it is necessary to trace the progress of the disease from its very beginnings. We will use a device called the Feeling Chart to illustrate what happens, when — and why. The Feeling Chart is simply a straight-line chart along which we can theoretically place every emotion the human being is capable of experiencing, ranging from pain to euphoria.

THE FEELING CHART

NORMAL

PAIN   EUPHORIA

Now let us imagine a character we'll call Ed. He is an average, normal sort of fellow — so normal, in fact, that he probably doesn't exist!*

---

* For purposes of simplicity, we have chosen to make our character a male. Of course chemical dependency is no respecter of either sex or sexual preference. We have also chosen to make him an *adult* male to avoid having to explain the various additional complications surrounding adolescent chemical dependency.

Finally, although this example illustrates alcoholism, the emotional syndrome holds true for *any* form of chemical dependency. Ed could just as well be using cocaine, marijuana, barbiturates, painkillers, or tranquilizers — *any* mood-altering drug.

One day Ed introduces himself to his first beverage containing ethyl alcohol. He is feeling okay already, the way he usually feels, but the drink causes him to feel even better — pretty good, in fact. Mood-wise, he moves in a welcome direction, from 1 to 2 on our Feeling Chart. He thinks, "This is great! How come I didn't know about this stuff before?" When the effects wear off, he moves back to where he started emotionally.

Ed has just entered Phase I of chemical dependency.

PHASE I: LEARNS MOOD SWING

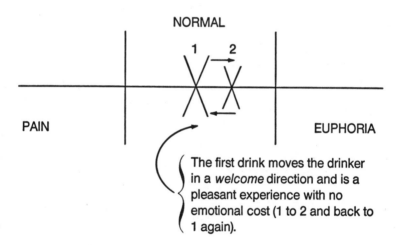

The first drink moves the drinker in a *welcome* direction and is a pleasant experience with no emotional cost (1 to 2 and back to 1 again).

Sooner or later, he makes a profound discovery: If one drink makes him feel good, then two (or three) are even better! He realizes that *he can control the degree of his mood swing* by controlling his alcohol intake. When that dosage wears off, he still returns to where he started from on the Feeling Chart, with no untoward effects.

PHASE I: LEARNS MOOD SWING

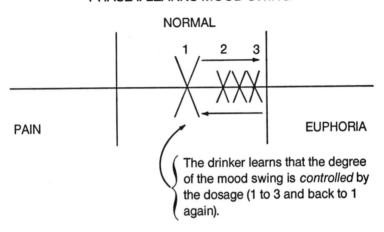

The drinker learns that the degree of the mood swing is *controlled* by the dosage (1 to 3 and back to 1 again).

Ed has had a significant learning experience, and these are the facts he has learned:

- Alcohol *always* moves him in the right direction — toward feeling warm, good-all-over, maybe even giddy;
- He can determine the degree of his mood swing by how much he drinks; AND
- It works every time!

It does not take Ed long to figure out how to select the mood he wants and drink just enough to get there. He accomplishes this *experientially* — by doing — and *emotionally* — by feeling. That, as anyone knows, is the best way to learn something new. Ed is not turning the pages of a textbook on drinking; he is bending his elbow, drink(s) in hand. Whether his drink of choice is beer, wine, or distilled spirits is irrelevant. Each takes him to the same happy place.

With time and experience, Ed comes to know that when he arrives home from work at the end of a long and tiring day, one drink always makes him feel a little better, while two or three enable him to put his cares aside. And with four, he feels terrific! He not only enjoys the mood swing, he actively seeks it. Again, he always returns to the mood he started from; he is not yet paying any emotional cost for his drinking behavior.

Ed is now in Phase II.

PHASE II: SEEKS MOOD SWING

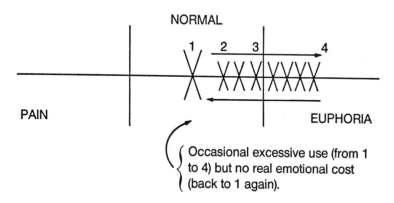

Occasional excessive use (from 1 to 4) but no real emotional cost (back to 1 again).

He has gone beyond knowing how to use alcohol to *forming a relationship with it*. This is a very positive relationship, one of implicit trust. Ed *believes* in the power of alcohol to relieve his stress, alleviate his worries, and dissolve his crankiness. He has graduated to the level of active social drinker — a card-carrying member of our drinking culture — and drinks fairly regularly and (usually) appropriately.

Given a little more time and experience, his relationship with alcohol becomes a deeply imbedded one which he will carry throughout his life. Experience builds on experience to strengthen and consolidate it.

He may stay in Phase II for weeks, months, or years. There is no way to predict how rapidly things will progress. Much later he may exercise hindsight and say, "I don't understand what happened. I used to have a lot of fun drinking. It's only been in the last two years that things have gone to hell in a handbasket." Like most chemically dependent persons, he will overestimate the period of happy using and underestimate the period when things went awry.

He may even get deliberately drunk on occasion, provided it's a special one that's worth painting the town for. He'll come home and announce to his wife, "Caroline, honey, I got that raise! Get dressed up; we're going out tonight." He overdoes it, and the next morning he awakens with a first-class hangover. His head is throbbing, his stomach is queasy, and he can't understand why he's so thirsty — he had plenty to drink the night before! But even from his bed of physical pain, Ed can look back emotionally and pay no price. He thinks, "Well, I really tied one on last night. I'm sure not going to do it again tonight! But I had a good reason, I had a good time, and it was worth it."

Many social drinkers never pass beyond Phase II. They continue to drink in appropriate places, at appropriate times, and in appropriate amounts. Drinking still moves them toward euphoria, and when the drinking has stopped they still return to normalcy (albeit with an occasional hangover).

Victims of chemical dependency, however, *always* move past this phase. In Ed's case, there comes a point at which his drinking behavior and excessive use begin to exact an emotional toll. This is the point at which he moves into harmful dependency, and it signals the true onset of the disease. *There is a direct correlation between the degree of emotional cost and the degree of dependency.* The higher the former, the more serious the latter.

How can we differentiate between so-called "normal" social drinking or drug use and harmful dependency? First, we must gather enough data about an individual's behavior to see whether the pattern has changed over time. Then we can begin asking questions.

1. Is there any indication of a growing anticipation of the welcome effects of alcohol or drugs? Does the individual seem preoccupied with those effects?

Ed walks through the door, tosses his briefcase on the table, and announces, "Boy, is it going to feel good to crawl around a dry martini! I need a drink; I've *earned* a drink."

He may adapt his behavior to ensure that he will be able to drink at a certain point (or points) during the day. He knows that he can't drink *all* day long, regardless of how it makes him feel; he realizes that alcohol is powerful stuff, and that he must limit his use. So he formulates a set of "rules" for drinking. One may be the "six o'clock rule": "I'll keep my nose to the grindstone during the day, but the minute I get home — at six o'clock — I'll have a drink."

Ed sticks to these self-imposed rules — for a while. But one day he catches himself looking at his watch. It's only four. Two more hours to go. Two more *long* hours to go. The next Saturday, when four o'clock rolls around, he's at home in front of the television set, or out mowing the lawn. He sees no reason not to have that beer *now*. What's the point in waiting until six?

By the following week he's checking his watch at noon. Lucky it's lunchtime. A glass of wine couldn't hurt.

Slowly, imperceptibly, Ed changes his lifestyle and his rules to satisfy his *growing* anticipation of the welcome effects of alcohol. He sees his coworkers drinking at lunch; he sees his neighbors downing beers while mowing their lawns. Everyone else is doing it, so he can, too.

Ed isn't aware that he has been rewriting his own rules until they are nothing like they used to be. Eventually he may do away with them altogether.

2. Is there a growing rigidity around the times and occasions when the individual has become accustomed to drinking or using drugs?

Does the person feel "put upon" if there is some unexpected interruption or intrusion upon his or her established routine?

Ed is halfway to the liquor cabinet when Caroline announces, "Dinner is on the table; remember, we've got that PTA meeting tonight."

Ed stops in his tracks and says, "What do you mean, dinner is on the table? I'm not ready to eat."

Caroline replies, "If you don't eat now, you won't have the chance. We have to leave in half an hour."

Ed, now irritable, counters with, "But this is when I relax!" (*Translation:* "This is my drinking time — hands off!")

Caroline says, "You can relax later, when we get home. You know I'm counting on you to be there; I'm making my presentation tonight."

Ed sighs. "I had a really hard day. I don't think I'm up to that meeting. I'd love to be there, but can't you go on without me? That will give me a chance to unwind, and when you come back you can tell me all about it. Okay?"

That scene will be replayed, over and over, in countless variations. Ed is not going to let *anything* interfere with his established drinking time.

3. Is the individual drinking or using more to achieve the same effects he or she formerly achieved with less?

Ed used to toss down one martini before dinner; lately he always has seconds. And sometimes thirds. But he *seems* like the same old Ed. Increased use of alcohol has resulted in an increased tolerance for its effects. The alcoholic who claims to be able to "drink everyone else under the table" often can, simply because it takes more to reach the mood shift he or she is seeking.

Another significant change takes place: Now there are times when Ed goes out of his way to get that second (or third, or fourth) drink. And this is why we ask:

4. How much ingenuity is the individual employing to get that greater amount?

You've been inviting Ed to your parties for years, but recently he has begun appointing himself bartender. He's the one who runs around saying, "Let me freshen your drink." Naturally this gives him ample opportunities to pour quick ones for himself. So while everyone else is nursing their second Margarita, Ed is on his third or fourth.

Caroline has noticed a difference, too. Before, she couldn't have paid him to do errands on Saturdays — going to the grocery store, picking up clothes from the cleaners, that sort of thing. Now he volunteers. He also usually includes a visit to the local watering hole somewhere along his route.

Ed is actually *planning* ways to get together with alcohol more frequently. Some of those ways are clever — ingenious, you might say. *The greater the ingenuity, the greater the dependency.*

He may or may not be secreting bottles in various nooks and crannies around the house, just to make sure that he doesn't "run out." Interestingly, this is one way in which most alcoholics are *not* particularly ingenious. They stash their bottles in much the same places alcoholics always have — out in the garage, down in the basement, in the bottom drawer of the built-in buffet.

Drug users have a somewhat easier time hiding their supplies, since they don't take up as much space as alcohol. And the person who finds them may not know the import of what he or she has come across. A marijuana joint can be tucked into a pack of regular cigarettes; mood-changing pills can be stored at the bottom of an aspirin bottle. Cocaine, to the uninitiated, looks like any number of ordinary household substances — baby powder, baking powder, powdered sugar. The discovery of drug-related paraphernalia is often the first sign a spouse or parent has that someone in the house is using drugs.

For Ed, Phase III is on the horizon. There comes a day when he drinks too much, exhibits some kind of bizarre behavior as a direct result, and *for the first time*, when he comes down from that mood swing, he slips back behind normal on the Feeling Chart. The next morning, as he reaches for the aspirin, he thinks about the night before and remembers the rude remark he made to the host, or the lampshade he wore on his head, or the fact that Caroline took the car keys away from him and insisted on driving them home. "What happened last night?" he thinks. "Booze usually doesn't affect me like that." He is uncomfortable, perhaps embarrassed. *He does not feel good.*

PHASE III: HARMFUL DEPENDENCY

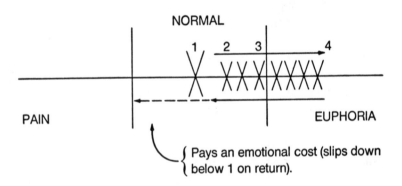

Pays an emotional cost (slips down below 1 on return).

Then — and this is critical — he immediately answers his own question: "Of course! I didn't eat before I started drinking; I drank on an empty stomach! The next time I drink that much, and I won't, I'll eat first."

Notice the ambiguity? He is already planning what he is going to do the next time he *doesn't* drink to excess!

Ed has committed his first rationalization. This is a reasonable, natural, caretaking response to a bruised ego; it is the human being's way of repairing damaged self-esteem.

A few additional words about rationalization are appropriate here.

- First, *all* people rationalize when their behavior has caused them some kind of legitimate discomfort. This is the function of rationalization: to help us feel better about ourselves when we have done something of which we're not especially proud.
- Second, *all* rationalizations must be unconscious in order to work. We cannot be aware that we're rationalizing as we're doing it; in fact, the more aware we are, the less successful our rationalization will be.
- Third, rationalizations are *positive* — as long as our ego strength remains at a normal level and we usually feel relatively good about ourselves. They make life easier.

When a *normal* person rationalizes to atone for feelings of failure, a dose of the facts is usually enough to bring him or her back through the rationalization to reality. ("Don't tell me I never mentioned dinner at my mother's. We talked about it last night, and I reminded you again this morning." "You're right. I guess I just didn't want to go.") But when the chemically dependent person rationalizes, it is a far different story. Rationalization becomes integral to his or her life. *Every* bizarre behavior is rationalized away, and the person is swept further from reality and deeper into delusion. The process grows increasingly rigid and actually helps to victimize the person as the disease progresses. The intellect continues to suppress the emotions and defend against reason until the truth is buried beyond reach.

We do not know *why* an individual slides into harmful dependency from the position of what appeared to be "normal" social drinking or drug use. But we can thoroughly describe the *how*, both behaviorally and emotionally.

It is worth emphasizing, over and over, that *the chemically dependent person remains utterly unaware of the progress of the disease.* As the behaviors become more bizarre, the rationalizations simply grow stronger to compensate for the increasing numbers of instances that exact an emotional cost. Rationalizations are no longer trotted out on occasion; they are part of the fabric of everyday life. They are invisible, they are insidious, and they are a necessary — and potentially disastrous — response to the feeling of pain.

The more the individual believes in his or her own rationalizations, the further into delusion he or she goes.

To the observer versed in the signs and symptoms of chemical dependency, Phase III is easily recognizable. It can be described, it has distinct symptoms, and it follows a predictable and progressive course.

For Ed, there comes another occasion of excessive use and even more bizarre behavior. The next morning, he not only feels uncomfortable; he experiences a twinge of *remorse*. He no longer wonders, "What happened last night?" He thinks, "What happened last night was stupid."

PHASE III: HARMFUL DEPENDENCY

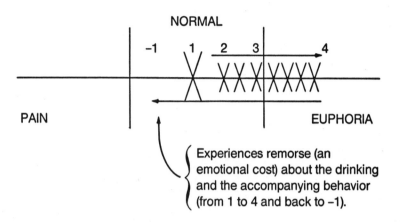

Experiences remorse (an emotional cost) about the drinking and the accompanying behavior (from 1 to 4 and back to –1).

As time goes on and he continues to drink excessively — maybe not every day, but often enough — his behavior goes beyond the bizarre to the outrageous, and his twinge of remorse becomes a stab. Now the morning-after reaction moves from "That was stupid" to "*I* was stupid. How could I have done such a thing?" The emotional pain is harder to bear.

Following the next bender, or the one after that, Ed slides into serious self-castigation. "I was stupid" is not sufficient anymore; now it's "I was a *fool*. I'd better call so-and-so to apologize." He feels awful. His self-worth is at an all-time low.

PHASE III: HARMFUL DEPENDENCY

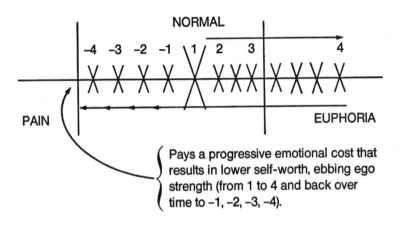

Pays a progressive emotional cost that results in lower self-worth, ebbing ego strength (from 1 to 4 and back over time to –1, –2, –3, –4).

And so goes the downward spiral, ever more painful and difficult to climb out of. Eventually this emotional distress becomes a *chronic* condition; Ed feels awful even when he is *not* drinking. This feeling may be an unconscious one, but it is always present. Initially it may be experienced as a general malaise; invariably, as Ed continues to drink and exhibit bizarre behaviors, it progresses toward sincere self-hatred. The aftermath of each new drinking episode echoes with self-recriminations: "I'm no damn good!" By this stage, Ed is a very sick man.

This is the point at which anyone who is paying attention will notice that something serious is going on. Personality changes and previously unseen mood shifts are evident — bursts of temper, violence, hostility, moroseness. The chemically dependent person may gain or lose weight due to improper eating habits. His or her personal hygiene may not be up to par.

PHASE III: HARMFUL DEPENDENCY

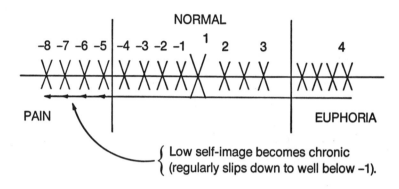

The typical response is to seek what we call the "geographic cure." At no time does Ed admit that his life is a mess because of his drinking; he doesn't admit it because *he still doesn't know it.* Instead, he assumes that the explanation lies in other people or other things. "That Caroline is such a nag; if I could dump her, I'd get better!" Or "I can't stand my job anymore. It's driving me to drink." Or "Maybe it's time to get out of this city — to start over. I need a change!" He may follow up these convictions with erratic actions.

His drinking is totally out of control. He drops into a bar for "a drink or two" after work — and is pushed toward the door at closing time. He brings home a bottle, planning to have a couple of short ones during the evening, and the next morning the bottle is empty.

In the final stages of this phase, self-hatred is replaced by clearly self-destructive feelings and attitudes. "I'm no damn good" is followed by "I'm so rotten that I might as well end it all."

Just flip the wheel at 60 mph and that bridge abutment will take care of everyone's problems, including mine . . . This office window is high enough; all I'd have to do is lean . . . Why open the garage door when I start my car? . . . I could take one or two of these pills — or I could take a handful . . . .

PHASE III: HARMFUL DEPENDENCY

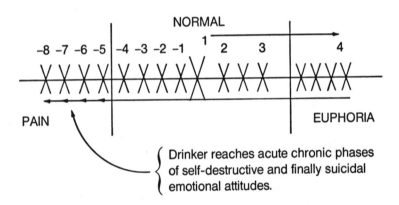

Drinker reaches acute chronic phases of self-destructive and finally suicidal emotional attitudes.

If the disease is allowed to continue, Ed may develop overt suicidal tendencies brought about by the chronic condition known as alcoholic depression — undoubtedly the largest single cause of suicide in our culture today.

Right now, you are probably asking about Ed (or the chemically dependent person in your life), "Why doesn't he see what is happening to him and quit drinking?"

Imagine the ten to twenty million practicing alcoholics who are behaving just like Ed. Now imagine the millions of people who know them and are noticing the same symptoms and behaviors that are evident in the person you care about. *They are all asking the same question* — and it is the wrong question.

To arrive at the right question, leave off the last three words. Then ask, "Why doesn't he see what is happening to him?" The answer is simple: *He can't.*

That may seem incredible on its face. How can a person who has changed his whole lifestyle not realize what he is doing? How can a person not be able to tell when he is centering his life around a drug? How can he not detect the deterioration in his physical condition, his emotional state, his relationships? Is he blind?

In a very real way, he is. The explanation is found in the emotional syndrome we are describing here.

As Ed's emotional need for alcohol has become more and more pressing, and as his drinking behaviors have been followed and reinforced by specific rationalizations, the very process of rationalization (which started out harmless enough) has become pathological *mental mismanagement.* His bad feelings about himself have been locked in at the unconscious level by a secure, high, and seamless wall of rational defenses. This is why he can believe what to everyone else seems patently unbelievable.

Because of the wall, he cannot get at those bad feelings about himself. He is not even aware that they exist. But they are nevertheless chronically present in the form of a *free-floating mass of anxiety, guilt, shame, and remorse.*

PHASE III: HARMFUL DEPENDENCY

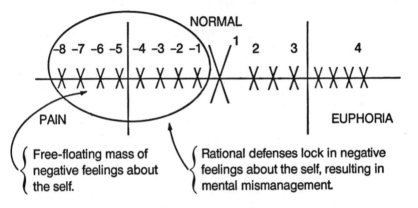

As long as he carries this free-floating mass inside himself, Ed can *never* feel good when he is not drinking, *and he does not even feel good when he is.* At this stage he can no longer achieve the happy "high" of the old days. *He drinks to feel normal* — and he enters Phase IV of the disease.

PHASE IV: DRINKS TO FEEL NORMAL

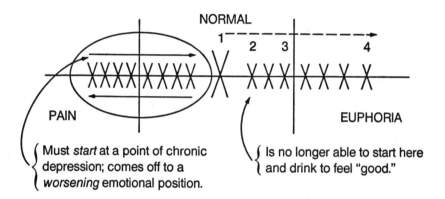

He starts drinking at a point below normal, where he is now living his feeling life. If he drinks enough, he feels the way he used to when he wasn't drinking. The terrifying thing about this phase is that each downswing takes him further and further to the left of the scale. He feels *worse* than he did before he consumed however many drinks it took to feel okay. Eventually he *must* drink because he simply cannot bear being sober. The resulting pain is searing, but it's worth it if he can feel normal even briefly.

As long as the disease continues, this free-floating mass keeps growing. Ed's self-image goes on deteriorating, his ego becomes more battered, and sooner or later rationalization alone is insufficient to do the job of covering up and locking in. At this point, another great defense system leaps to the cause, equally unconsciously. We call this system *projection*.

Projection is the process of unloading one's self-hatred onto others. Like rationalization, it must be unconscious in order to be effective.

Ed sees himself as surrounded by hateful people. If *they* would shape up, *he* would be all right! His boss is a pain, Caroline is a nag, the kids are driving him crazy, the neighbors are bugging him, his mother is pushing him to the limit. He starts dumping his bad feelings onto them.

**PHASES III AND IV: HARMFUL DEPENDENCY
AND DRINKING TO FEEL NORMAL
LEAD TO PROJECTION**

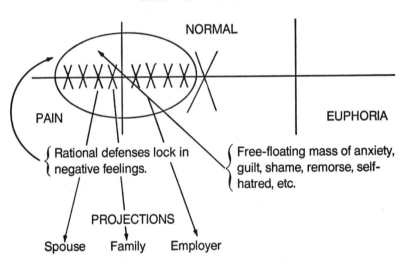

What he *seems* to be saying is, "I hate you all!" What he is *actually* saying is, "I hate myself." But *he* doesn't know this, and *you* don't know this, and besides, you're caught up in some powerful bad feelings of your own.

How Chemical Dependency Affects You

We have a saying: "Alcoholism *includes* alcoholics." What it means is that the people around the chemically dependent person — spouse, children, employer, neighbors, friends — are also vulnerable to the effects of the disease.*

This book assumes that you are close to the chemically dependent person about whom you are concerned. Precisely because of this closeness, you have symptoms of your own to deal with. This book also assumes that you are not a practicing alcoholic or drug addict. Precisely because of this distance, you should be able to recognize and come to terms with these symptoms.

---

* Let us not forget the most innocent of victims: the unborn children of alcoholic or drug dependent mothers.

There is now ample evidence that drinking during pregnancy — even in very moderate amounts — can damage the developing fetus and result in an undersized, retarded, and/or physically deformed baby. Alcohol is one of the three most common causes of mental retardation in the United States today, and it is the *only* one of the three that is *entirely preventable.*

The only safe course is for the expectant mother to avoid alcohol and drugs altogether, unless under specific instructions from her doctor. It is also recommended that she abstain while nursing.

For more information on alcohol and pregnancy, write:

> National Clearinghouse for Alcohol Information
> PO Box 2345
> Rockville, MD 20852

Or call (301) 468-2600.

Request copies of *Should I Drink? Think First of Your Unborn Child* and *Preventing Fetal Alcohol Effects.* Both are free.

In addition, the Johnson Institute has a pamphlet available on this subject, "Drinking and Pregnancy: Preventing Fetal Alcohol Syndrome." For more information, call 1-800-231-5165. In Minnesota, call 1-800-247-0484.

Your relationship with the chemically dependent person has given rise to a number of unpleasant and confusing feelings. See which of the following sound familiar to you. Most apply to the members of families in which one or more people are chemically dependent, but some are also relevant to coworkers, neighbors, and friends.

Anger

It may seem as if you are involved in a "love/hate" relationship with the chemically dependent person. You love him or her, but you hate what you are going through because of that person's dependency. At times you feel angry and resentful.

One cause of your feelings until now has been your inability to separate the person from the disease. Perhaps you were not even aware that chemical dependency is a disease, and not a chosen condition. What you have just learned should help you to make that separation and view the situation from a less clouded perspective.

You would not get angry with the person for coming down with the flu. Instead, you would offer to help, because you would want the person to recover.

Intervention is a way to help an individual recover from the disease of chemical dependency. It is a positive, constructive, achievable series of actions you can take to ensure that he or she gets better.

Shame

During some of the painful experiences that have resulted from the dependency, you may have felt ashamed of the person. Perhaps his or her behavior has been so inappropriate or outrageous as to embarrass you in front of others. Perhaps you have even been ashamed of *yourself* — for associating with the person, and for being powerless to do anything about his or her behavior. Shame is contagious; it tends to produce low self-worth in everyone it touches.

Hurt

Emotional pain can be broad and deep. It is painful to see someone you care about change as harmful dependency progresses. It hurts to become involved in arguments, or witness angry exchanges between that person and others. And it *really* hurts when the person blames *you* for his or her dependency. "If you'd get off my back, I'd stop drinking!" "You want to know why I drink? Look in the mirror!" "All you care about is yourself. If you paid some attention to me, maybe I wouldn't need to drink." Accusations like these cut to the core.

Fear and Uncertainty

It can be frightening to live or work with someone who is chemically dependent. You can't count on the person; you never know when the next big scene will erupt; if you are financially interdependent, there may be real cause for concern about how and when the bills will be paid. If the person is prone to violent outbursts of temper, you may even fear for your physical safety.

And what about the future? Will things keep getting worse? Or — and this prospect can be equally frightening — will they stay the same?

Loneliness

The stress involved in relating to a chemically dependent person results in a breakdown of normal communication. Love, respect, and mutual concern are lost in the crises of day-to-day living. The isolation created by the lack of nurturing, rewarding interaction leads to a deep and abiding sense of loneliness. You may feel cut off, rejected, unwanted, unloved.

The Desire To Be Perfect

Spouses and children of chemically dependent persons tend to take on specific behaviors in an attempt to shield themselves from the anger, shame, hurt, fear, and loneliness that come from being in a dependent family situation. One of these is the striving for perfection — what we call "being too good to be true."

Here are some of the most obvious "being-too-good" behaviors:

- Achieving for the family — in school, at work, in sports, in the community.
- Doing more than one's share around the house.
- Counseling the family and/or attempting to patch up family fights and relationships.
- Being cute, funny, and entertaining at inappropriate times in an effort to relieve stressful situations.
- Not allowing yourself to make mistakes; denying those you do make.
- Intellectualizing about the situation — permitting yourself to *think* about it, but never to *feel*.
- Parenting (even if you are not a parent): disciplining the other children in the family, worrying about family finances, acting as parents to other adults.
- Trying to meet everyone else's expectations and keep them happy.
- Being rigidly obedient; *always* following *all* the rules.

Is there anything wrong with "being too good?" Unfortunately, yes. These behaviors work to insulate the chemically dependent person from having to experience the harmful consequences of his or her dependency. Your constant striving for perfection actually *enables* him or her to continue being dependent.

"Being too good" perpetuates the illusion that the family does not have a problem. It, too, is a form of rationalizing, of covering up, of pretending that nothing is wrong.

Rebelliousness

The other side of the "being-too-good" coin, rebelliousness is also a form of enabling. Here are some typical rebellious behaviors seen in chemically dependent families:

- Being dishonest.
- Being late for work.
- Acting out in school and at home.
- Breaking house rules.
- Defying authority at home, at school, or on the job.
- Starting arguments with family members or neighbors.
- Being a bully, playing hurtful pranks or tricks.
- Bossing other family members, coworkers, or a neighbor's children.
- Rejecting your own family and developing a "family" of friends of whom your parents (or spouse, or children) do not approve.
- Neglecting your own family members or becoming verbally and/or physically abusive.

Rebelliousness effectively draws attention away from the chemically dependent person and his or her inappropriate behaviors. It also helps to disguise the pain you are feeling as a result of those behaviors.

Apathy

Another feeling prevalent among people who are involved with chemically dependent persons is the apparent *lack* of feeling. Here are some common apathetic behaviors:

- Withdrawing from the family.
- Being habitually quiet; not offering opinions of any kind, whether critical or supportive.
- Cutting oneself off from others.
- Passively rejecting the family.

- Excessive indulgence in fantasies or daydreams.
- Passively rejecting *all* relationships, both within and without the family.

Apathy may look like calmness, serenity, a philosophical attitude toward trouble, or acceptance of the situation. Inside, however, you are suffering the same turmoil and anxiety that everyone else is experiencing.

Like "being-too-good" and rebelliousness, apathy enables the chemically dependent person to progress further along in his or her disease.

Guilt

We have found that almost everyone who has anything at all to do with a chemically dependent person feels some sense of guilt, large or small. This guilt may stem from the conviction that one is powerless to help, or the belief that anything one tries to do to help is somehow wrong. (After all, the chemically dependent person certainly doesn't welcome any helpful overtures!)

But its *primary* source is usually the notion that one is somehow responsible for the chemical dependency. This is part of the delusional system that the disease creates to protect itself.

▶ Chapter 3 ◀

THE DELUSIONAL SYSTEM
OF CHEMICAL DEPENDENCY

We have already discussed how rationalization and projection work together to block the chemically dependent person's awareness of the disease. By keeping the alcoholic or drug addict out of touch with reality, they eventually make it impossible for him or her to understand that a problem exists.

From the outside, it appears as though the person is lying. (We often hear alcoholics characterized as liars — even *pathological* liars.) The people around the chemically dependent person assume that he or she is still responsible to the truth and capable of knowing it and distinguishing it from falsehood. They can't understand why he or she doesn't simply face up to the problem and do something about it.

While rationalization and projection are sufficiently devastating psychological impairments in their own right, three new progressive (and even more bewildering) conditions enter in during the later stages of the disease. *Blackouts*, *repression*, and *euphoric recall* literally *destroy* the person's ability to remember what has happened during any given drinking or using episode. What used to be mental mismanagement evolves into a full-scale *faulty memory system*, or delusional system.

What We Know About
the Delusional System

A faulty memory system is typical of the disease of chemical dependency and is almost universally present in sufferers. It is also one of the hardest things for people around them to comprehend.

Blackouts

If any of us experienced a period of time when we walked and spoke and made telephone calls and parked the car, and later couldn't remember any of it (even after talking to witnesses), we'd go at once to a doctor for a thorough checkup and an explanation. But chemically dependent persons sense that blackouts are part of their drinking or using — and it's a part they don't want to examine too closely. Instead, they adapt, learning ways to cover up these occurrences, and they continue to drink or use drugs despite them. *The willingness to tolerate repeated blackouts as a normal part of life rarely if ever occurs in the absence of chemical dependency.*

A blackout is a *chemically induced period of amnesia.* This should not be confused with passing out — the total loss of consciousness that sometimes occurs as a result of excessive drinking or drug use. During blackouts, people may continue to behave and function in an otherwise normal fashion, and everyone around them assumes that they are in complete control of their faculties. It is only later that the truth emerges. Victims are unable to recall anything about the blackout period — *and never will.*

Alcoholics and drug addicts experiencing blackouts have driven cars, flown commercial airplanes, performed surgery, and tried and argued court cases. They have traveled to foreign countries, arrived back home without knowing how, made appointments, done household tasks, and carried on at parties.

In short, *any* activity a person can do can be performed during a blackout.

The quantity of alcohol or drugs consumed seems to have no direct relationship to the frequency or duration of blackouts. A small amount may cause one while a large amount may not, and vice versa. A blackout may last for seconds, minutes, hours, or days.

As these memory losses occur, victims become increasingly fearful, bewildered, and depressed. With the progression of the disease, the memory losses become more frequent and unpredictable. Anxieties begin to mount. ("What did I do last night after 10 o'clock?" "Where did I leave the car?" "Who was I with?" "Where did I hide that bottle?")

Because chemically dependent persons cannot remember what goes on during blackouts, they are denied the specific feeling reactions to the bizarre, antisocial behavior which often occurs during them. In some instances, even blackouts are "blacked out." Large periods of time are totally unaccounted for. Guilt, shame, and remorse are vague and nameless and of no help in self-recognition — as the accurate recall of drinking behavior would be.

One recovering alcoholic used these words to explain the sick feeling that follows a blackout: "I thought I was going crazy. So every time this happened to me, I'd force myself to forget it. I got so good at it that I actually had myself believing that things just 'slipped my mind' from time to time." Another recalled, "I used to think that everyone drew a blank once in a while, when he had drunk too much."

Since the anxiety resulting from a blackout is so great, alcoholics or drug addicts will tend to minimize, discredit, or disbelieve any firsthand accounts of their behavior during blackouts. "My wife (or husband) is always exaggerating these things," they will say to themselves — and eventually accept as the truth. This conflict between what others say about their behavior, and what they will *allow* themselves to believe, contributes to a growing feeling that others are being "unfair" about their drinking or drug use. The delusional system cooperates with them to blunt the truth and aid in their ongoing denial of the disease. The eventual result is widespread confusion.

Let's return to our friends Ed and Caroline to illustrate these points. One night Ed and Caroline go to a party at the home of their good friends, Stan and Elizabeth. Midway through the evening, Ed makes a pass at the hostess. Everyone in the room sees and hears it — including Caroline.

The next morning Ed ambles downstairs for breakfast. Caroline is furiously frying eggs and slamming cabinet doors. Ed walks into the kitchen, sits down at the table, and picks up the newspaper — business as usual. A moment later he casually remarks, "Nice party last night. Did you enjoy yourself?

Caroline is stunned. The very least she had expected was an apology. And there's Ed with his nose in the newspaper, asking her if she had a good time!

"Don't you *remember*?" she asks accusingly.

Ed looks up. "Remember what? I remember driving over, helping Stan fix the drinks, sitting down to dinner, eating, joking with the neighbors, and coming home to bed."

"You made a pass at Elizabeth," Caroline says. "Right in front of everybody. I wanted to die then and there. How *could* you?"

Ed squirms without quite knowing why. "What do you mean, how could I? I couldn't! I didn't! Caroline, I would never do such a thing. You must have been dreaming."

Now Caroline is faced with two awful possibilities. Either Ed is lying outright — or maybe she *was* dreaming. She discards these and moves on to a third: Ed is a cad who doesn't even have the decency to apologize.

Later that day, Ed calls Stan, hoping to borrow his lawn-mower. For the first time in their long acquaintance, Stan is chilly over the telephone. Ed doesn't understand it. Unless . . .

No, that's impossible. He *couldn't* have done that terrible thing of which Caroline accused him.

But he can't remember anything that happened between dinner and coming home.

Repression

While repression results in forgetfulness similar to that caused by a blackout, it is *psychologically* rather than chemically induced.

Over time, chemically dependent persons develop the ability to repress unwanted, shameful memory material. They literally shut it out of their minds. They continue to rationalize some of their behaviors (those they can bear to face), and they repress those they cannot rationalize.

Like rationalization, repression is a human survival skill. None of us could endure the memory of *every* shameful or embarrassing moment we've experienced during our entire lives; the sheer enormity would overwhelm us. When a *normal* person represses a specific memory, it is usually of no great consequence, since the behavior that led to the memory is unlikely to be repeated. But when a chemically dependent person represses, it is because those actions that produced the pain and shame have occurred more than once and are likely to recur and worsen with the passage of time.

The more bizarre the behavior becomes, the stronger the instinct to repress. Outward manifestations of this can be seen in intensified nervousness, resentment, hostility, and self-pity, and eventually self-destructive and suicidal emotional tendencies.

Also like rationalization, repression becomes counterproductive, even destructive, when it is allowed to go too far. It works to push the chemically dependent person deeper into the disease until the truth becomes virtually unattainable — unless it is brought back forcibly through intervention or a fortuitous grouping of crises.

Let's assume that Stan and Elizabeth are forgiving people, and that they invite Ed and Caroline to their next big bash. Ed's behavior is even worse this time. Not only does he flirt rudely with Elizabeth; he insults Stan, pours a pitcher of martinis over Stan's boss, and manages to break a valuable heirloom while stumbling toward the kitchen.

On awakening the next day, Ed is glad to find himself in his own bed. No telling where he might have ended up! He tries to get out of bed — and sinks back down on the pillows. He has the worst hangover of his life. But it's Saturday, and he's told Caroline that he would run some errands, and he'd better, if only to make up for the fact that he went on a bender the night before . . . he had *promised* her that he wouldn't. So he crawls out of bed, into his clothes, and down the stairs.

Along the way, he is overcome by a feeling of pure horror. He doesn't remember much of anything that happened last night; he just senses that it was *bad.* His unconscious goes to work. It can allow all the memories of the night before to surface . . . or it can close them off, bury them, repress them. In a split second, the decision is made. Note that this is not premeditated, but instinctive; Ed's mind is already heading in a new direction, away from the sheer awfulness of those memories. Ed is thinking about washing the car, doing some shopping, buying Caroline a dozen roses.

Meanwhile Caroline is beside herself. She isn't even cooking breakfast; if Ed wants to eat, he can find the stove. Instead, she's nursing a cup of coffee and wearing a face like thunder.

Ed strolls into the kitchen and Caroline's resentful glare. What's going on? His beloved wife, the light of his life, looks like hell. Chances are she's about to start in on him again. Maybe he can head her anger off one more time. So he walks over to her, wraps his arms around her, gives her a big smile, and asks, "Is something bothering you?" He feels neither shame nor guilt nor remorse, because he can't imagine any reason why he should. He truly wants to help her, to make her feel better.

She pushes him away, bursts into tears, and runs out of the room. Ed is flabbergasted. Upstairs, behind a locked door, Caroline is weeping and pulling her hair. How *could* he be so calm, so collected. so kind? How could he pretend that last night never happened? Unless . . . perhaps . . . it was all in her head.

Euphoric Recall

The third component of the delusional system may be the most devastating; it is certainly the most difficult to comprehend and accept. Most people have some understanding of blackouts. All of us have some familiarity with repression. But euphoric recall seems patently incredible!

What it does is to make it impossible for chemically dependent persons to evaluate their current condition accurately while under the influence. They *really don't know* that they can't do everything they're capable of doing under ordinary circumstances. Their subsequent memories of the experience are tied into the inability to evaluate their condition. And those distorted memories are *implicitly trusted.*

Picture the man who is obviously quite intoxicated, yet heads toward his car with his keys at the ready. He perceives himself as perfectly capable of driving home. Everyone else sees that he's *in*capable and highly dangerous, but they can't convince him. When someone finally does manage to take his keys away, he reacts with indignation and sincere bewilderment.

The next morning, while reviewing the events of the previous evening, he *remembers* that he was all right — just as he believed he was the night before. Regardless of what his wife or friends may tell him, he trusts this memory implicitly.

Chemically dependent persons who are victimized by euphoric recall remember how they *felt*, but not how they *behaved*. They have no memory whatsoever of slurred words, exaggerated gestures, or the fact that they wove around the room. They *felt* as if they expressed themselves brilliantly and entertained everyone with their wit and humor, and that is what they are positive happened.

One woman listened in disbelief to a tape recording of one of her drinking episodes. Before playing it back, her husband asked her if she could remember *how* she had said *what* she had said on the previous night. "Of course I can," she replied. "I had a few drinks, but I was perfectly coherent." She was convinced that this was the case — until she heard her own voice stuttering, stammering, and slurring through the virtually nonsensical statements she had made the night before. "Then it hit me," she said. "How many times had I remembered *feeling* good, when I had actually *behaved* like a complete idiot?"

One man put it this way: "When I used to tell people that 'I just wasn't myself' last night or last week, I thought I was using a figure of speech. But it was the truth!"

Chemically dependent persons who have progressed to the late stages of the disease remember *every one* of their drinking or using episodes euphorically. Although they are incapable of recalling any of the details, they firmly believe that they remember everything. And what they remember most clearly is how good they felt while they were drinking.

Anyone who dares to argue with them is a nag or a party-pooper or just plain wrong. "Whaddaya mean, I already told that joke? You're just jealous because you can never remember a punch line." "You won't dance with me because I step on your feet? Nonsense; I'm a terrific dancer. Maybe I should give you some lessons!" "Don't be ridiculous; hand over the keys. I'll drive."

Imagine how many drunk drivers are on the road every night, convinced that they're in full control of their faculties.

Let's return to Ed and Caroline once more. Ed can't understand why the two of them are never invited to Stan and

Elizabeth's parties. He'd heard about one just last week, and it sounded like a lot of fun. That Stan is a real spoilsport. Who needs him?

Plus there's this ongoing argument he's having with Caroline. Lately, whenever they go out together — and they don't do that too often anymore — she insists on driving home. He gives her the keys to humor her, but he wishes she'd lay off. He's always been a careful driver, and except for that one DWI he didn't deserve, there's never been a time when he couldn't run circles around every other car on the road.

As if hassling with Caroline weren't enough, his boss is all over him about his production. Apparently you can't please anyone these days. Ed is working as hard as ever, maybe harder, despite the fact that he isn't feeling that well. The doctor says it's his liver, but that's impossible. Drunks have liver trouble, not people like Ed.

And here is where we leave him — with his friends falling away, his marriage in jeopardy, his job on the line, and his health failing. Everything is going to the devil around him. Good thing *he* doesn't have any problems.

How You Become Part of the Delusional System

You are having a conversation with your spouse, and this is what he or she is saying: "I remember quite clearly what happened last night, and I don't understand why you're always exaggerating. I was perfectly all right. Why can't you ever have a little fun at a party, like I do? Why can't you loosen up?"

But what about the slurred words, the weaving gait? "What about them? I was walking okay; I was talking better than the radio announcer. That's how I remember it; that's how it *was*."

What is it like to live with someone like that? He or she looks you straight in the eye and says, "What you are saying never happened. It never happened that way." And your reaction is, "Maybe it didn't. Maybe *I'm* going crazy."

When you spend a great deal of time with an individual who is trapped in the delusional system, it is easy to get caught up in it yourself. How can you believe that you love a liar and a drunk?

Rationalization, repression, and euphoric recall combine to keep the chemically dependent person genuinely and sincerely out of touch with the severity of his or her symptoms. They are hard to bear and almost impossible to comprehend. But for many family members and friends of alcoholics, projection is the unkindest cut of all. Projection results in what concerned others cannot help but perceive as personal attacks, and they hurt.

- "If you weren't so boring, I wouldn't find drinking so fascinating."
- "Maybe if you'd put a decent meal on the table once in a while, I wouldn't have to eat at the corner bar."
- "Can't you shave and get a haircut? You look like a bum. And you insist on trying to cram your fat stomach into those pants . . . You're really disgusting."
- "Those kids would drive anyone to drink. Can't you do something about them? What kind of parent are you?"
- "If you'd gotten that promotion, maybe we could have nice things and take a vacation once in a while, like the neighbors do. You've never been any good, and I don't know why I married you."
- "My mother was right about you. She said I'd be making a big mistake if I ever got mixed up with you, and I sure did."
- "If you were more of a woman, I wouldn't need to drink so much."
- "If you were more of a man, I wouldn't need to drink so much."

As you absorb the brunt of these defenses, your self-image progressively deteriorates. You, too, fall victim to defenses of your own, which are essentially the same as those of the alcoholic.

In most cases, the spouse or other loved one takes on one or more of the following roles. See if any ring true for you.

The Protector

During the initial stages of the disease, when the chemically dependent person's drinking or using episodes occur infrequently, you unconsciously assume a lifestyle which causes you to adopt the defensive attitude of the *protector*. This thrusts new responsibilities upon you, including:

- making apologies to family and friends for the person's antisocial behaviors;
- calling his or her employer to make excuses for alcohol-or drug-related absences or tardiness; and
- supporting the various rationalizations he or she makes to deal with his or her drinking or drug use.

Each time you are forced to accept one of these new responsibilities, your self-image drops another notch and your defenses rise to conceal reality from you. Your own rationalizations and repressions cause you to believe that "It really is the flu" or "Last night wasn't all that bad." Like the defenses of the chemically dependent person, yours form a wall of self-deception which allows the disease to progress and worsen.

Slowly but surely, these defenses gain control of your life. As the person's compulsive drinking or using increases, so do his or her spontaneous projections. You become the recipient of more and more accusations, recriminations, and reprisals.

Although the chemically dependent person is really dumping

his or her self-hatred on you, you don't know this. Instead, you feel even more guilty and inadequate. You question your worth as a spouse, a parent, a person. You seriously wonder whether *you* are the cause of the problem.

As your self-doubts intensify, your own defenses rise once again, this time to block the reality of the drinking or drug use and hide your negative feelings about yourself. Not only are you protecting the chemically dependent person; you are protecting what is left of your own self-image and integrity. You feel compelled to prove that you are still a meaningful and worthwhile human being. So you try to be the *ideal* spouse, the *ideal* parent, the perfect person.

You continue to nurse the chemically dependent person, apologize for him or her, make excuses, and support his or her other reasons for drinking or using. You successfully deceive yourself into thinking that "Everybody drinks too much once in a while" and "If I change somehow, this will all go away"

The Controller

As the drinking or drug abuse and projections continue, your sense of self deteriorates even further. You feel an increasing responsibility for the other person's behavior. Your declining self-worth strengthens your growing belief that somehow *you* are the cause. In an unconscious attempt to regain some feelings of worth, you adopt the attitude of the *controller*. You take on new behaviors, including:

- drinking with the alcoholic (or doing drugs) in the hope of limiting his or her intake;
- cancelling any social events which might result in excessive drinking or drug use;
- buying the liquor or drugs yourself in order to keep such purchases under control;
- pouring out or hiding extra quantities of liquor, or flushing the drugs away;

- pleading that if he or she loved you and the children, he or she would stop drinking or using (or at least cut back);
- taking over the family finances.

The chemically dependent person's projections send you the constant message, "If it weren't for me, there wouldn't be a problem." His or her drinking or drug use becomes an outward manifestation of your own internal inadequacy. Your feelings of self-worth are directly tied to his or her drinking or drug use; in other words, *you* can't feel good about yourself until *he or she* does something about the problem.

You are caught in a downward spiral. The more you attempt to control the chemically dependent person's alcohol or drug intake, the more he or she consumes. The more he or she consumes, the more inadequate you feel. The more inadequate you feel, the more compulsively you try to control his or her drinking or drug use. And so it goes, becoming ever narrower, more constrained, more terrifying.

The Blamer

In a vain and desperate attempt to handle your now constant and ever-growing feelings of low self-worth, you incorporate the role of *blamer* into your wall of self-deception. You start to project your feelings of failure, hurt, fear, and anger onto others — most often the chemically dependent person, since he or she seems to be the cause of all of your troubles.

- "If you would just drink like other people, I wouldn't be such a nag."
- "If you would use a little will power, you could control your drinking or drug use. I control mine!"
- "Oh, sure. Another flat tire. Just like the one you had last week, and the week before."
- "If you don't do something about yourself, I'm taking the kids and leaving."

- "Either you stop drinking (or using), or this marriage is over."

Of course, you don't always use words . . . a cold shoulder and glaring eyes are equally effective.

As the disease progresses, you experience more uncontrollable and inappropriate mood swings. You fluctuate between extended periods of deep depression to violent outbursts of rage and hostility that are often triggered by minor irritations. These mood swings leave you feeling bewildered and convinced that you are going mad. Your defenses come to the rescue and block the full impact of these feelings — which in turn keeps you from gaining the necessary insights which could free you from your prison of anger and despair.

The Loner

Gradually you lose any ability to improve your own self-esteem. You are locked into a self-defeating pattern of relating to others which now affects all areas of your life. Other family members and friends begin to feel uncomfortable with you because you are constantly slipping into defensive roles.

- "I'm the only thing that's holding this family together."
- "Why can't you be more like . . . ?" "I told you so!"
- "What I put up with for the children's sake . . ." "What a life I could have had, if only . . ." "What's meant to be, is meant to be . . ."

The result of such behavior is the increasing alienation of your family and friends. You begin to feel as if you are totally alone in the world.

The Enabler

In the end, your own defenses are so highly developed that you cannot see how they are working to make matters worse. By assuming more and more responsibility for the chemically dependent person — through the roles of *protector*, *controller*, and *blamer* — you are transformed into a full-fledged *enabler*.

Your behavior allows the chemically dependent person to avoid the consequences of his or her abnormal drinking or drug use. Your compulsive and desperate attempts to manipulate and control his or her drinking or using actually *support* it.

The end result is the continuation of a progressively worsening situation. Both you and the chemically dependent person become ever more angry, isolated, and alienated.

The Co-Dependent

Unless the disease of chemical dependence is arrested and *you get help for yourself* as well, you move from enabling into *co-dependency*. Like the chemically dependent person, you are out of touch with reality and unable to see how your own defenses keep you locked in a life of hostility, self-pity, and loneliness. You continue to pick up the pieces after each episode while growing more protective, controlling, and blaming. And you continue to hide reality from him or her — and from yourself.

You are now suffering from essentially the same disease. It is predictable, progressive, and chronic, and it may be fatal.

There is another role available to you, a role that can reverse this process of deterioration and lead toward recovery for you and the chemically dependent person. That is the role of the *intervener*.

Before discussing this, let us look briefly at two other common approaches that invariably prove ineffective: *inappropriate confrontation* and *sympathy*.

One wife, when asked if she had ever confronted her husband about his condition, snapped back, "There isn't anything left in the house to throw at him!" To her, confrontation meant throwing things. But while this may have temporarily eased her frustration, it did nothing to help her husband.

He already felt so bad about his drinking that, consciously or unconsciously, he believed that he *deserved* to be punished. Whenever his wife accommodated him, he was able to replace his guilt feelings with self-pity and resentment — and go on living with his addiction.

A group of recovering alcoholics who had been sober for periods ranging from a few months to a decade or more was asked to examine in retrospect what persons were most helpful in causing them to recognize their alcoholism. What had these persons done? How had they broken through the wall of defenses?

The data revealed that most "confrontations" were superficial and evidenced only a shallow understanding of the dynamics of alcoholism. Rather than being confronted with their condition as a progressive, deadly disorder affecting their entire lives, these recovering alcoholics recalled being told things like, "Maybe you ought to quit drinking. You don't seem to be able to handle it like you used to." Their usual response, supported by the well-developed defense system of chemical dependency, was equally superficial: "I can handle it just as well as before, or better than you can."

As long as their condition is related *only* to times or quantities or behaviors connected with drinking or using, chemically dependent persons encounter no serious threat to their defenses. They have handled these situations countless times.

They can remain relatively comfortable while saying, "Doesn't everybody make the same mistakes?" *They do not see themselves as different from most other normal or healthy people* who "also go off the deep end occasionally and have other troubles, too."

What is needed is a breakthrough to reality. But this breakthrough can be delayed or prevented when unknowledgeable concerned persons resort to inappropriate cofrontation — or to sympathy. Sympathy might make *them* feel better, but all it does for the people they are trying to help is to reduce their anxiety level. They are able to live with their dependency less painfully and, therefore, less realistically. Both approaches delay the moment of truth which only intervention can achieve.

The Intervener

The successful adoption of this positive role begins with an understanding of the nature of chemical dependency. By learning about the disease, you can reduce some of the irrational guilt you feel about the chemically dependent person's condition.

You must also become aware of the extent of your own co-dependency. Your compulsive reactions have blocked many of your own negative feelings about yourself and kept you from coming to terms with them. These defenses weaken once you start to identify and examine them whenever they arise. As many of your previously hidden feelings emerge and become available to you, you can explore and alleviate them — and realize that *you are not responsible for what is happening to the chemically dependent person*. With your self-worth removed from his or her drinking or using, you can avoid the trap of spontaneously reacting to the disease and instead develop the freedom to choose a useful and meaningful response to the individual and the illness. That useful and meaningful response — intervention — is the topic of the second part of this book.

As you begin reading Part II, you will see that intervention takes time. It cannot be accomplished overnight, and you should not attempt it until you feel ready. But there *are* two things you can do, starting *now*.

1. If you are in the habit of inappropriately confronting the chemically dependent person, STOP.
This will deprive him or her of a major rationalization for drinking — and the punishment he or she feels is "deserved" and gives him or her permission to drink or use again.

2. If you are accustomed to protecting the chemically dependent person, STOP.
Leave him or her alone to deal with the consequences of drinking or using — even problems with the law. The disease will then become more exposed to him or her, and more vulnerable to intervention.

Finally: As you start learning about and preparing for the intervention, be aware that help is available for you, too. At some point you may want to consider seriously seeking treatment for yourself, and part of the up-front work you will be doing prior to the intervention may well show you where to find it. Your *immediate* and *primary* concern, however, should be that of helping the chemically dependent person. His or her need is even greater than yours, and it becomes more urgent with each passing day.

PART II

INTERVENING WITH CHEMICAL DEPENDENCY

▶ Chapter 4 ◀

PREPARING FOR
THE INTERVENTION

Intervention is a process by which the harmful, progressive, and destructive effects of chemical dependency are interrupted and the chemically dependent person is helped to stop using mood-altering chemicals and to develop new, healthier ways of coping with his or her needs and problems. It implies that the person need not be an emotional or physical wreck (or "hit bottom") before such help can be given.

There is a shorter, simpler way to define intervention: *presenting reality to a person out of touch with it in a receivable way.* We have explored the various defenses with which the chemically dependent person shields himself or herself from the painful and debilitating reality of his or her disease and its effects. The goal of the intervention is to break down those defenses so that reality can shine through long enough for the person to accept it.

By "presenting reality," we mean presenting *specific facts* about the person's behavior and the things that have happened because of it. "A receivable way" is one that the person cannot resist because it is *objective, unequivocal, nonjudgmental,* and *caring.*

An intervention is a confrontation, but it differs in some very important respects from the sort of confrontation with which most people are familiar — and which have little or no positive effect.

In an intervention, confrontation means compelling the person to face the facts about his or her chemical dependency. It is not a punishment. It is not an opportunity for others to clobber him or her verbally. It is an attack upon the victim's wall of defenses, not upon the victim as a person.

Similarly, an intervention is an act of *empathy* rather than sympathy. You agree to take part in it out of the deep concern you feel for the chemically dependent person. You stop *caring for* the alcoholic or drug addict — and start proving how very much you *care about* him or her.

For the chemically dependent person, the intervention is the "moment of truth." He or she experiences it as a crisis, a discrete event. In fact, it takes days, even weeks, of advance preparation. *The better prepared you are, the more smoothly the intervention will go.* The only "surprises" during the process should be those the victim experiences when finally met head-on with the realities of his or her disease.

Conquering Your Own Reluctance

You may need to start by convincing *yourself* that intervention is the best approach, and the best time to begin the process is *now*.

It is normal to approach intervention with reluctance or even fear. You may worry that it will only make things worse. You may feel despondent, as if nothing will help and nothing will ever change. You may feel angry and resentful. You may be so weary of the whole situation that you're not that interested in helping.

Following are some questions you may be asking yourself — and some answers that should motivate you to take action.

"Why now?"

The longer you delay, the longer the person will suffer — and the more life-threatening the disease will become. Permanent disability (including brain damage) and even premature death are inevitable unless the destructive process is successfully interrupted. The sooner this happens, the more likely it is that the person will recover.

Studies indicate that those alcoholics whose illnesses resulted in the more severe physical, economic, and social disorders had more difficult and prolonged recoveries. On other hand, there's evidence that where physical health has *not* been broken, jobs have *not* been lost, and families have remained intact, alcoholics have tended to recover more often and more quickly.

"Why me?"

If you have read the first part of this book, you know quite a bit about chemical dependency — probably a great deal more than most of the other people surrounding the person. As a result, you can play an especially important role in the process by educating others about the disease.

Besides, if not you, then who else? Has anyone approached you about the need to intervene with the person? If not, it may be due to their own entrapment within the delusional system. It is possible that they can no longer see the disease for what it is, if indeed they ever could. Or they may be waiting for "something to happen" to change the situation.

You are aware of how dangerous it is to wait. If nobody else is taking action, and if you truly care about the person, then you *must* take immediate steps to halt the progress of the disease.

"I've heard of people who simply turned themselves in for treatment. They seemed to realize all at once that they had a problem. Can't that happen to the person I know?"

It's possible, but not probable. What you're wondering about is something we call *spontaneous insight*, which isn't really spontaneous at all.

The emotional syndrome and the delusional system of chemical dependency combine to make it virtually impossible for the chemically dependent person to admit or even recognize that he or she has a problem. Once in a while, and this is *very* rare, so many things will go wrong at the same time that a piece of reality slips through the wall of defenses. (In retrospect, the recovering person will claim that "everything went to hell in a handbasket.") These *fortuitous groupings of crises* prove so overwhelming that the person practically flees into treatment. Life reaches such a critical point that he or she may pick up the phone and call for help, or go to detox, or join A.A.

But this doesn't always happen, and you can't afford to gamble on it. Remember that we are talking about *certain premature death* if the disease is not arrested.

People who reach this point — those who have been saved by fortuitous groupings of crises — are those who have gotten the sickest. At the Johnson Institute, our goal is to reach the "up and outers," not only the "down and outers." Early intervention is the way to accomplish this.

"I'm not married to the person — we're just friends. Won't intervention look like interference in his or her private life?"

This is a genuine concern for some people. Most of us were raised to be polite, to respect others' privacy, and to mind our own business. We hesitate to be rude, or cruel — both of which intervention seems to require.

It is not rude to help a sick person; it is not cruel to save someone's life. In fact, intervention is a profound act of caring.

"Intervention seems so secretive — even sneaky. I don't like the idea of going behind someone's back."

Intervention is the opposite of secretive. In truth, it helps everyone — from each concerned person who participates, to the chemically dependent person himself or herself — finally to break the "rule of silence" under which they have all been living.

It's a great relief for the spouse or child or neighbor or coworker to be able to talk about what he or she has seen and experienced. At last, everyone can tell it like it is!

First, however, certain preparations must be made. The group must be organized into a process. Where, when, and how the chemically dependent person will be approached must be decided. All of this must take place without unnecessarily arousing the person's defense systems, which are already pathological. The overriding goal is to reach the person when he or she is most likely to listen, *and to hear.*

Revealing the nature of these preparations should be part of the intervention. On that occasion, you might say something like this: "We've all been having a tough time for the past few weeks. We've been meeting about you, and we've wanted to take you into our confidence, but we couldn't just yet. Finally, today, we can." Or: "We're going to share everything with you now. We haven't been going behind your back; instead, we've been getting it all together so we can share it appropriately and usefully."

If you are concerned that the person might become angry or defensive, keep this in mind: Countless numbers of recovering alcoholics have later said, "Thank God someone knew enough and cared enough to do this for me!"

Gathering the Intervention Team

The intervention should be conducted by a team comprised of two or more persons who are close to the victim and have witnessed his or her behavior while under the influence. The chemically dependent person's defense systems are far too highly developed to be breached by one person acting alone.

There are many advantages to doing it in a group. First, the victim immediately realizes that the situation is serious when he or she is faced by several people all saying essentially the same things. It is fairly easy to discount or dismiss the claims of one person (especially if that person has tried before to introduce the subject of the drinking or drug use); it becomes harder when these claims are made by a chorus. A group carries the necessary weight to break through to reality.

As the old saying goes, "He will laugh if one person tells him he has a tail. If three people tell him, he may turn around to look!"

Second, it can be reassuring and strengthening for *you* to have supportive company during this potentially painful event. The chemically dependent person is bound to react with a variety of negative responses, and it's best if you don't have to bear their weight by yourself. And third, more people can present more evidence that a problem exists. Unless you have been with the victim during every second of the disease, you haven't seen it all!

Thus the intervention process begins by gathering a team of people who, like you, sincerely want to help.

STEP 1: Make a list of meaningful persons other than yourself who surround the chemically dependent person.
The key word here is *meaningful.* These should be persons with whom the victim has a fairly close relationship, whether by necessity or by choice. They should exert a strong influence upon the victim, since his or her denial will sweep aside the efforts of others.

They should *not* be chemically dependent themselves. People who have not come to terms with their own disease are unlikely to want to point out the symptoms in someone else, even if they are capable. And the chemically dependent person is not likely to stand for the pot calling the kettle black!

If the person is married and you are not the spouse, then the spouse (or significant other) should be at the top of your list. He or she can help you to determine other potential group members from among the following:

- the chemically dependent person's employer or immediate supervisor

It can be *extremely* helpful to have the employer or supervisor as part of the intervention team. In our society, people's identities center around their jobs. Chemical dependents often cling to their job performance as the last bastion of respectability as the disease brings the rest of the world crashing down around their ears. They use it as "proof" that they can't have a problem: "I've never missed a day's work in my life because of drinking." (An honest look at their performance usually destroys this myth!) Sometimes the employer is a more effective intervener than a family member or a friend, simply because he or she holds such an important card.

- the chemically dependent person's parents

It is most convenient if they live in the area. Even if they do not, however, you may want to consider getting them involved.

Siblings are other good possibilities, again depending on geography.

- the chemically dependent person's children

Children can be a valuable part of the intervention team; in most cases, they are well aware that a problem exists. As a very *general* guideline, we recommend that the children asked to participate be at least eight years old. They should be able to verbalize their feelings and describe the behaviors they have seen (and the disappointments they have experienced).

Adults often wonder if children will be frightened or upset by the intervention. Chances are that they have already been touched by the effects of the disease on their parent. In the intervention setting, they will finally have the opportunity to speak out and be supported by other adults. This can be a great relief, especially if they have been covering up their own feelings of fear, confusion, rejection, and hurt.

There is another way in which children tend to benefit from an intervention: Educating them about the disease can help them to understand it better, and this in turn can actually strengthen the relationship between them and the victim.

● close friends or neighbors of the chemically dependent person

While the chemically dependent person may socialize primarily with a group of "drinking buddies" or drug users, there may still be old friends "left over" from the pre-disease days, or new friends who are not heavy drinkers or users. These two criteria will help you to decide which to invite into the group: 1) Does the person listen to them and respect their opinions and viewpoints? 2) Have they been around the person during drinking or using episodes, and have they witnessed instances of bizarre or unusual behavior? In other words, do they have firsthand knowledge of how the disease is affecting the person?

The victim's self-delusion can usually be penetrated only by those whose approval or esteem are essential to his or her self-image. On an emotional level, this most often means members of the immediate family and the employer. Often, however, friends may be especially effective in helping the person to face his or her behavior. He or she may have been able to rationalize that the drinking is only the symptom of a family problem. Hearing from an observer who is outside the family circle may help to destroy this rationalization.

● coworkers

These should be people with whom the victim works on a regular basis; perhaps they share the same office or have cooperated on a long-term project. Again, the victim should respect them, and they should have firsthand knowledge of the situation.

● a member of the clergy

If the victim attends a church or synagogue, the pastor, priest, or rabbi can be a vital part of the team, as long as he or she personally possesses useful information. This can either be firsthand knowledge of the victim's behavior, or extensive experience in working with other chemically dependent persons.

STEP 2: Form the intervention team.

Now you must contact the people on your list and ask them to participate in the intervention. (If your list has turned out to be quite long, you may want to narrow it down. A large group can be unwieldy. In fact, our experience has shown that groups of 3-5 seem most effective.)

The best team members are those who *know something about chemical dependency*, *are willing to risk their relationship with the victim*, and *are emotionally adequate* to be interveners.

The friend or coworker who insists that alcoholism or drug addiction is a sign of "moral weakness" will not be much help during the intervention. Each member of the team should have sufficient knowledge about or insight into chemical dependency to:

a) accept the definition of addiction as a disease in which "normal" willpower is inadequate to control the use of the chemical;
b) realize that the effect of the chemical itself further reduces the strength of even "normal" willpower;

c) realize that the victim, because of the need to explain away his or her behavior, has developed a defense system so effective that it results in a high degree of self-delusion — including the inability to recognize the true nature of the disease;

d) understand that because of this degree of self-delusion, the victim is *absolutely unable* to look at his or her behavior with a clear eye, which is why help must come from the outside; and

e) realize that chemical dependency isn't just a bad habit — and that the victim is going to live or die based on what happens during the intervention and afterward.

You may find yourself doing some educating. Simply by reading the first part of this book, you have learned a great deal about chemical dependency. Share this information with prospective team members.

Expect some resistance, especially when it comes to making the commitment to play an active role in the intervention. People will be glad to talk to *you* about the person's drinking or using and how they feel about it (especially if they feel personally affronted or wounded by it), but it's another matter entirely to put their relationship with the victim on the line. That can be frightening.

A spouse will say, "I agree, my husband has a problem, but if I do what you're asking he'll divorce me!" A friend will say, "She'll never speak to me again. I'll lose her friendship for sure." A child will say, "Daddy gets mad when I talk about his drinking." A supervisor will say, "We're so busy that I don't know if I can afford to rock the boat. And what if she turns around and claims discrimination or some such thing, and raises the roof with my boss?"

You can counter each of these arguments in various ways. For example, with a young child, it's often enough to explain that Daddy (or Mommy) is very sick and needs help *soon*. Many companies today have at least some insight into the widespread problem of chemical dependency; some even have counselors on staff to assist employees.

But the ultimate argument is the simplest. *If they do nothing, the chemically dependent person will die prematurely.* It all boils down to two choices: They can intervene, thereby risking their relationship with the person (which is already deteriorating as a result of the disease), or they can do nothing and watch him or her continue to die slowly but surely.

The final criterion is emotional adequacy. Intervention should not be attempted by people who are so distressed that they might harm themselves or disrupt the process. Similarly, it should not be attempted by those who are immobilized by fear, or so full of rage toward the sick person that they cannot see beyond it.

Gathering the Data

There are two types of data you should compile in preparation for the intervention: facts about the victim's drinking or using behavior, and information about treatment options.

STEP 1: Make written lists of specific incidents or conditions related to the victim's drinking or drug use that legitimatize your concern.

This is something that *each* member of the intervention team should do. Even children can write out lists or ask adults for assistance in putting what they have experienced into their own words.

These lists should be written in the second person, since they will be read aloud to the victim during the intervention. ("*You* did so-and-so," not "My husband did so-and-so.") And they should be *very* specific. Generalizations — "You drink too much," "You have to stop drinking," "Your drinking is getting worse," "You're away all the time" — are useless and even harmful, since they are felt as personal attacks.

Each item should explicitly describe a particular incident, preferably one that the writer observed firsthand. Here are some examples:

- "Last Thursday night at 8:00 you came in slurring your words and knocked over and broke the lamp on our living room table. Perhaps you do not remember that because you had obviously been drinking."
- "On Monday, when I went to do the laundry, I found another empty bottle in the basement clothes hamper."
- "Last month we had to break a dinner engagement three times in a row because you had been drinking so much during the days."
- "Jim talked to me after the meeting on Friday and told me how concerned he's getting about your drinking. You insulted the speaker and several guests, and he had to drive you home."
- "Our neighbors mentioned this morning that they've noticed how withdrawn you've become this year. They wonder if there's any way they can help."
- "Do you remember falling down in the bathroom at 2 a.m. last Saturday morning? When I went to see what all the noise was about, I found you sprawled on the floor. There was liquor on your breath."
- "On Monday night I looked out my window and saw you passed out on your front lawn. It was 20 degrees outside, and I was worried about you."
- "Last month you charged $300 worth of liquor on our credit card."
- "A week ago you stayed home from work for three days in a row, claiming you had the flu. But it was really because you were too hung over to get out of bed."

- "On Monday night you told me you'd come straight home from work. Instead, you came in at 1 a.m. and slept in your clothes, which smelled of alcohol."
- "Last week I came home to find the children outside by themselves. You were asleep on the couch, and there was an empty liquor bottle on the floor beside you. The children were hungry and frightened. Susie said she'd tried to wake you up and couldn't."
- "You lost the car twice last month after you'd been out drinking. I had to drive around parking lots trying to find where you'd left it."
- "When you picked us up from school, you drove so fast that me and my friends were scared. And you said a lot of things that didn't make sense."
- "You promised to come to my class play, and then you got sick again. I was really disappointed."
- "Sam had to cover for you on Tuesday when you didn't get back from lunch until three in the afternoon. When you did arrive, you were slurring your words."
- "At the office party, you had four drinks in a row and then spilled your fifth all over somebody. I was embarrassed for you and worried that you might lose your job."

Each incident should be described in unsparing detail. The more incidents that each group member can list, the better.

The age of technology may have brought us the ultimate intervention tool: the camcorder (video camera). As these are becoming more affordable, more families are buying them. Nothing has quite as much shock value — and is harder to deny — than a full-color, stereo videotape of the alcoholic weaving around, slurring his or her words, and generally behaving inappropriately. If you have a camcorder, use it!

STEP 2: Find out about treatment options in your area.

The ultimate goal of the intervention process is to get the person into treatment or some other form of continuing care. You should be prepared to suggest this at the intervention itself — and to offer specific recommendations. It is wise to make an advance reservation at a treatment center or clinic; if the wall of defenses crumbles, the victim may be willing to go then and there.

There are several sources to consult. You may want to start by calling your family doctor for advice. Or visit your local library. One book you may find useful is *Roads to Recovery*, edited by Jean Moore (New York: Macmillan, 1985); she lists several hundred residential treatment facilities nationwide and provides brief descriptions of each.

Or check the White Pages of your telephone directory for the following:

- Alcoholics Anonymous (A.A.)
- (Your city, county, or region) Committee on Alcoholism or Council on Alcoholism
- Division on Alcoholism, Public Health Department
- Division on Alcoholism, State Health Department
- (Your state) Department of Mental Health
- (Your state, city, or county) Medical Society

In the Yellow Pages, look under "Alcoholism Information and Treatment Centers," "Family Service Organizations," and "Mental Health Clinics."

If you cannot find what you need locally, then write or call the following, stating your needs and asking for referrals:

The Johnson Institute
510 First Avenue North
Minneapolis, MN 55403-1607
Telephone: 1-800-231-5165
In Minnesota, call: 1-800-247-0484

Employers can learn about Employee Assistance Programs and other on-the-job programs to help employees deal with alcoholism from:

Association of Labor-Management Administrators and
  Consultants on Alcoholism, Inc. (ALMACA)
1800 North Kent Street
Suite 907
Arlington, VA 22209
Telephone: (703) 522-6272

Division of Occupational Programs
National Institute on Alcohol Abuse and Alcoholism
Department of Health and Human Services
5600 Fishers Lane
Room 11055, Parklawn Building
Rockville, MD 20857
Telephone: (301) 443-1148

If the person is a veteran, contact:

Alcohol and Drug Dependence
Mental Health and Behavioral Science and Services
Department of Medicine and Surgery
Veterans Administration
8 Vermont Avenue NW, Room 116A3
Washington, DC 20420
Telephone: (202) 389-5193

Once you have a list of possibilities, *find out more.* Request copies of brochures or other publications. Ask for complete program descriptions. Do they have an aftercare program? What percentage of their patients are still recovering after one year? two years? ten years? Does the program stress treatment of the entire family through A.A., Al-Anon, Alateen, Narcotics

Anonymous, or a similar group that integrates the principles of the Twelve Steps? And — importantly — does the program consider intervention a viable and worthwhile approach? Some do not.

Don't rest until you have at least one treatment option that seems workable. *You are not ready to do the intervention until you have performed this critical task.* When interventions do not result in victims accepting care, it's because the intervention team is unprepared in this area. If the chemically dependent person does express willingness to go into treatment, and you can't respond with a name, address, and telephone number, then the wall of defenses may well rise up again, stronger than before And your other efforts will have been in vain.

Rehearsing the Intervention

It is recommended that you conduct one or two "rehearsals" — practice sessions — prior to the actual intervention. These should be attended by everyone who will be at the intervention, with the exception of the chemically dependent person. Each member of the intervention team should come prepared with his or her written list of facts about the chemically dependent person's behavior.

Rehearsals perform several functions in addition to the obvious one of preparing team members for the intervention.

- They help family members and other concerned persons to realize that they are not alone — that others have been affected, too.
- They provide a forum for mutual support and understanding.
- They alleviate tension and fear and reduce the likelihood that people will say unclear or unfocused things, or things they never really meant to say.

- They require team members to focus on their choices and the possible outcomes of those choices.
- They establish a climate for change and inspire the belief that it *is* possible to do something about the problem.

You may want to devote part (or all) of your first rehearsal to reviewing the characteristics of the disease of chemical dependency. (See pages 5–10 of this book, "What We Know About the Disease.") Give people a chance to ask questions and share what they know.

When you are reasonably sure that all team members have some understanding of the disease and its effects, you are ready to move on.

STEP 1: *Designate a chairperson.*

Team members should agree on one person to "direct" the rehearsals and the intervention itself. If the victim's employer or immediate supervisor is part of the team, there are two good reasons why he or she might be your first choice: his or her management experience, and the fact that he or she is *not* a family member. Spouses and adult children who have suffered a great deal of emotional pain as a result of living with the chemically dependent person are usually not suited for this role.

The chairperson's primary responsibility will be ensuring that the intervention does not turn into just another family row. Thus, team members should also agree to follow his or her direction. When the chairperson says, "All right, Mary, it's time to let Fred have his say," then Mary should give the floor to Fred.

STEP 2: *Go over each item on the written lists that team members have prepared.*

Team members should read their lists aloud, one item at a time, and each item should be either approved by the team or revised as necessary.

Remember that these should be *specific* descriptions of incidents or behaviors that are related to the chemically dependent person's use of alcohol or drugs. They should be totally honest and as detailed as possible. They should be devoid of value judgments, generalizations, and subjective opinions.

Be alert to overtones of self-pity or hostility — emotions that can block communication and turn the intervention into a shouting match or a stalemate. The *only* emotion present in these statements should be one of genuine concern.

If children need to be coached in reading their lines, take this opportunity to help them. Resist the urge to put words in their mouths; it's preferable if they say things in their own way and don't sound as if they're parroting the adults on the team.

Reviewing team members' lists is important for two reasons. First, it gives people the chance to "get their stories straight" — to figure out exactly what they want to say and how they want to say it. And second, it works to break the "rule of silence."

There is a pattern that is typical of almost every chemically dependent situation, whether at home or on the job. As the victim moves into increasingly bizarre or destructive behaviors, there are usually several witnesses. But they tend not to share what they know with one another. They are afraid that doing so will hurt the victim, or they hesitate to speak out because of some kind of misplaced loyalty to him or her. Whatever the reason for their silence, it works to support the sickness — to enable it to progress and worsen.

Many an intervention rehearsal has been interrupted by cries of "I didn't know you knew that!" or "I thought I was the only person who noticed that!" Some secrets turn out not to be so secret after all. Others, revealed at last, work to strengthen team members' sense of commitment. As more than one person has said, "If I had known even half of what I've heard tonight, I would have done this sooner!"

STEP 3: Determine the order in which team members will read their lists during the intervention.

Someone will have to go first! And second . . . and third. Determining the order ahead of time will prevent awkward pauses and keep the victim from interrupting or sabotaging the process.

It is best to start with someone who has a close and influential relationship with the chemically dependent person and stands the greatest chance of breaking through the wall of defenses. Often the best choice is his or her employer or supervisor.

Don't rely on memory for this step; the chairperson should write down the order and bring this record to the intervention, prepared to remind people as necessary that their turn has come.

STEP 4: Choose someone to play the role of the chemically dependent person during the rehearsals.

Although this is not required, it can be extremely helpful. One purpose of the rehearsals is to give team members a feel for what the real intervention will be like — all the way down to the probable objections, denials, excuses, and outbursts from the person for whose benefit the intervention is being done.

You may want to pass this role along from one team member to the next, giving everyone a chance to voice the objections, denials, excuses, and outbursts he or she may already have heard from the chemically dependent person. The point is to be aware of these and prepared to respond to them. It is highly unlikely that the victim will sit through the entire intervention without saying a word; it's best, therefore, to anticipate what he or she will say and decide ahead of time precisely how to respond. This leads us to the next preparatory step.

STEP 5: Determine the responses that team members will make to the chemically dependent person.

The decision to take part in the intervention represents only part of the commitment that each team member must make. Now is the time to discover just how far people are willing to go and what they are willing to do to convince the victim to accept help.

A wife may say, "I've had it with him. If he doesn't get help, he can move out — or I'll take the kids and go." Does she mean it? *Will* she take the kids and go? Does she have somewhere to go to? Has she said all this before, and let it pass?

A supervisor may say, "Her production is way down, and she's having a harmful effect on her coworkers. They've been complaining to me about their extra workload. If she doesn't enter treatment, I'll have to fire her." Can he do this? Will he?

A neighbor may say, "I've put him up on my living-room couch for the last time. Unless he gets help, my door stays closed." Does he mean it? The next time the victim shows up and pleads for a place to sleep, will the neighbor turn him away?

A child may say, "I'm not getting in the car anymore when Mom is driving. She scares me when she's drunk. From now on, I'll get rides from my friend's parents, or I'll stay home." Will she stick to it? Are there friends she can call for rides? What if she can't find anyone to drive her someplace she desperately wants to go?

Most people involved with the chemically dependent person will be accustomed to giving ultimatums — and equally accustomed to backing down. That process must come to an end.

Responses must be both *realistic* and *firm*. If the wife isn't genuinely prepared to take the kids and leave, she shouldn't say that this is what she plans to do. The supervisor should find out precisely what his company's policy is on chemical dependency, determine an action (or series of actions), and be ready to follow through.

What if the victim stands up and threatens to walk out during the intervention? Someone must be prepared to say, "Please sit down and hear us out." What if he or she verbally attacks a team member midway? That person must be prepared to continue reading his or her list anyway, all the way to the end. What if the victim bursts into tears and vows to reform? While it's tempting to accept such a vow on face value and stop the intervention then and there, it isn't at all wise to do so. The team should be prepared to move on to the conclusion — the point at which everyone has had his or her say, and the chemically dependent person is told that he or she must accept help of some kind.

Each action on the part of the chemically dependent person must be met with a reaction that is in keeping with the tone and purpose of the intervention. If the most appropriate reaction is an ultimatum, the person who delivers it must be ready to carry it out.

STEP 6: *Conduct the rehearsal.*

The rehearsal — and the intervention itself — should begin with a simple and empathic introductory statement from the chairperson. It might go something like this:

> "_____ (the name of the chemically dependent person), we're all here because we care about you and want to help. This is going to be difficult for you and for us, but one of the requests I have to start out with is that you give us the chance to talk and promise to listen, however hard that may be. We know it's not going to be easy for the next little while . . . Would you help us by just listening?"

Notice that this statement clearly establishes the chemically dependent person's role as *listener* — and the intent of the group to keep him or her in that role.

Next, the team member chosen to go first should read through his or her written list. The person who is playing the part of the chemically dependent person may now bring his or her acting skills to the fore. What is he or she likely to say? How is he or she likely to behave? Most team members already will have had some sort of confrontation with the chemically dependent person; they may even be able to quote him or her. ("What do you mean, I have a problem? *You're* the one with the problem. If you'd quit nagging me, I'd quit drinking!") Practice responding with, "Please listen to what I have to say . . .," followed by more from the lists.

Each team member should have the opportunity to read through his or her lines and predict how the chemically dependent person may react. Meanwhile, the chairperson should serve his or her primary function of keeping team members on track. A rehearsal can be awesomely true-to-life; it is not unusual for team members to revert to accusations or generalizations, or to get carried away by their emotions. That is why each person should also practice expressing his or her caring and concern for the victim of the disease.

Try preceding each complaint with a positive statement: "Honey, you've always been a great husband, but I'm worried about you. Last week, when you'd been drinking, you drove right through the garage door . . ." "Mom, I really appreciated all the effort you put into my birthday party. But I was really embarrassed when you fell over the chair. I knew you were drinking wine instead of punch . . ." "Howard, your coworkers like you a lot. Everyone says that you're always willing to help out in a pinch. But you've been coming back from lunch later and later with alcohol on your breath, and last week I saw you sleeping at your desk."

The intervention process assumes that reality will break through somewhere along the line. At some point, the chemically dependent person will "see" his or her life *as it really is* — perhaps for the first time in years. Those who have participated in interventions describe the remarkable changes that take place. The room is permeated with a feeling of relief, and often of love. Team members are simultaneously exhausted and filled with hope. Any anger the victim may have been feeling is replaced by shock and anguish, and sometimes profound embarrassment. More than one has looked around the room and said, "My God, I didn't realize I had hurt you all so much. I'm sorry!"

While this may feel like the end of the intervention, it is only the end of the *first stage.* It is equally important to rehearse what comes next: insisting that the victim agree to accept help, and presenting the available options. The options, which you will have carefully researched, should be narrowed down to *this* hospital, *that* treatment center, or, in some cases, outpatient counseling and A.A. Allowing the victim to choose from among them will help to restore some measure of his or her dignity.

Of course, there is always the possibility that he or she will insist that treatment is unnecessary because a decision to stop drinking has been made from the heart. You know that it can't last, so you should be prepared to try an alternate approach. (We call it the "What If" response.) "You've made that decision before. Go ahead and try. But *what if* you take even one more drink? Will you agree to accept help then?"

In all probability, the victim will make a sincere effort to stop drinking on his or her own. But *just because a person stops drinking does not mean that he or she starts recovering.* The disease — including the emotional syndrome — is still present and as virulent as ever. This results in what is commonly called the "dry drunk."

What are the signs of a dry drunk? Irritability, anxiety, nervousness, resentment, and self-pity, to name a few. The person may overreact to simple frustrations, be hypersensitive or hypercritical, and generally behave unpredictably. Often the people around him or her will yearn for the good old drinking days, when the person was easier to live with!

In other words, while abstinence is an important goal, it is not the *only* goal. In truth, it is a single step, albeit a significant one, on the road to leading a full and fulfilling life once more. Stopping drinking by itself creates a vacuum, and living in that vacuum can be pure hell.

The central goal of recovery — and of the kinds of care that promote it — is the restoration of the victim's ego strength. The *whole person* must be treated, and that includes the mind *and* the body. The chemically dependent person suffers emotionally, mentally, and spiritually as well as physically. The best treatment programs available today recognize this, and they make use of interdisciplinary teams that include psychologists, psychiatrists, chemical dependency counselors, social workers, members of the clergy, physicians, and nurses.

Thus the second stage of the intervention — which you should practice as thoroughly as the first — involves eliciting a firm agreement from the victim to accept help. You *must* be prepared with one or more concrete suggestions: "You have an appointment to see Dr. So-and-so right after we're through here; I'll drive you." Or: "We've reserved space for you in such-and-such a hospital. I already have your plane ticket, and your bag is packed and waiting in the car."

Try to anticipate as many objections, excuses, and well-meaning promises as you can — and prepare a firm response to each.

With so much work to do prior to the actual intervention, it's easy to see the necessity for one or more rehearsals. In fact, you may conduct as many as you wish; the more prepared you are, the more able you will be to deal with the realities of the situation. Just remember that time is of the essence. The sooner you arrest the progress of the disease, the sooner the victim can begin the process of recovery.

Finalizing the Details

When will the intervention be held? Schedule it for a time during which the chemically dependent person is likely to be sober. It's best if this is also a time soon after a drinking or using episode — for example, a Saturday morning following a regularly scheduled Friday night out. If the person is feeling under the weather as a result, that could work to your advantage, since his or her defenses will be proportionally weakened.

Where will the intervention be held? Choose a place that won't arouse too much anxiety in the victim, since you do not want to raise his or her defenses. It should also be a place where there will be no interruptions.

Who will be responsible for ensuring that the chemically dependent person arrives at the intervention site? That person should say only what is necessary to cause the person to attend.

Will anyone else need help getting there? Who will call the others to remind them of the time and place?

Which team member will ask the chemically dependent person for the commitment to listen to what the team has to say? Who will make the necessary arrangements for the person to go into treatment, provided that he or she agrees to accept help immediately? Who will explain the treatment and recovery plan?

Leave nothing to chance — not even the most minute detail. You will never again have the element of surprise so completely on your side. Use it!

Should You Seek Professional Help?

The Introduction to this book expresses the Johnson Institute philosophy that *anyone who sincerely wants to help, can help.* Chances are you're quite capable of doing an intervention without the assistance of a qualified professional. However, *if you feel the need for such assistance, you should seek it.*

Thanks in large part to the widespread interest in chemical dependency today — combined with the growing awareness of the magnitude of the problem in our society — trained and capable helping professionals can be found in most areas of the country. If you do not know where to look, start with the resources noted on pages 74–75. Any reputable social agency, mental-health center, or other alcohol facility should be able to provide you with a list of names and telephone numbers.

It is recommended that you conduct an initial face-to-face interview with any professional with whom you are considering working. Find out the following:

- Does he or she recognize chemical dependency as a disease?
- Does he or she support and believe in the intervention process?

Those who do will forgo the classic counseling approach — "Do you think you could get the person in to see me?" — and focus instead on assisting those people who can intervene more effectively.

- Has he or she had firsthand experience with interventions?

If the answer to all three questions is "yes," you are on your way toward a productive relationship.

There are many excellent reasons to enlist the aid of a professional counselor, especially one who will commit to the entire process. To begin with, a counselor's position outside the circle of those who are directly involved with the chemically dependent person can ensure objectivity. A counselor makes a good chairperson and may also be skilled at playing the part of the chemically dependent person during rehearsals; he or she has probably seen and heard all (or most) of what you will witness during the intervention.

A counselor can provide valuable input during the gathering of data, ranging from going over team members' lists to recommending available treatment options. He or she will also be trained to alleviate team members' fears and anxieties about the intervention.

Finally, the counselor can help you and the other team members to understand how living, working, or closely associating with a chemically dependent person can lead to the parallel symptoms of co-dependency. He or she can also help you to understand and come to terms with your own enabling behaviors — and identify your own needs for treatment and recovery.

A few words of caution: At the Johnson Institute, we have grown concerned in recent years over the tendency of some counselors to prolong the intervention process. While they conduct one preliminary meeting after another with the chemically dependent person's family members and friends, the disease rages on unabated. Two to three educational and practice sessions are acceptable and even advisable, but there is seldom a need to undergo several months of counseling or preparation prior to the intervention. Afterward, perhaps, but not before; your most pressing goal should be that of arresting the disease, and the best time to do that is as soon as possible. Your counselor should have the same goal and the same sense of urgency.

Chapter 5

DOING THE INTERVENTION

If you have completed the steps described in Chapter 4, you are as ready for the intervention as you will ever be.

In other words, it's time to act. You now have the ability and the resources to arrest the disease of chemical dependency and help the person you care about to start on the road to recovery.

You may be nervous. You may be fearful. You may be worried about the unpleasant scene you suspect will ensue. But your overriding feelings at this point should be those of commitment and genuine concern.

As you prepare to walk through the door to wherever the intervention is to be held, take a moment to congratulate yourself for going as far as you have. You have made the effort to learn about the disease and how it is affecting you; you have undertaken the arduous and painful task of looking back at the person's behaviors and seeing them for what they are; and you are willing to put your own relationship with him or her on the line. The Good Samaritan himself could have done no more.*

An Intervention Scenario

No one can tell you precisely how to conduct your intervention. There are simply too many variables: the condition of the chemically dependent person, the stage to which the disease has progressed, the personalities of the team members, the dynamics of the interpersonal relationships, how much the team members know about chemical dependency, the presence (or absence) of a trained professional, the treatment options available, and so on.

We can, however, walk you through a scenario that represents some of the events that may occur during an intervention. While no intervention is "typical," the following should be fairly representative of what goes on.

---

* There are some very special circumstances when a team comprised of laypersons should *not* attempt to do an intervention.

It is strongly recommended that you seek professional help before proceeding should any of the following apply:

- The chemically dependent person has a history of mental illness;
- His or her behavior has been violent, abusive, or extremely erratic;
- He or she has been profoundly depressed for a period of time; or
- You suspect polydrug abuse but lack sufficient information or eyewitness accounts of the victim's actual usage.

We have noted that the person must be sober during the intervention But while it is fairly easy to recognize the signs of alcohol consumption, the presence of other drugs or combinations of drugs may not be as obvious. Some have been known to produce psychotic or near-psychotic states. *If you cannot be certain that the individual is chemically free at the time the intervention is scheduled, wait and seek professional help before trying again.*

The person about to be intervened upon is our old friend, Ed. His wife, Caroline, has spent the past several weeks learning about chemical dependency — reading books and articles and talking with friends who have chemically dependent loved ones. She had an especially long conversation with her sister in another city, whose husband has been recovering for five years.

She also had a private meeting with Ed's supervisor, Bob. After reviewing company policy, Bob has agreed to take a hard line with Ed and insist that he accept treatment. The company's insurance will cover it, and Ed's job will be waiting for him when he returns.

This is the intervention team that Caroline has gathered:

- Bob, who will also serve as chairperson;
- Melanie, Ed and Caroline's 24-year-old daughter
- Tom, their 16-year-old son
- Howard, a neighbor and close friend to Ed

The intervention is scheduled for 10:00 on Saturday morning in Bob's office. Bob has asked Ed to come in to prepare for a report that is due to a client on Monday. He will arrive at 10, and Caroline, Melanie, Tom, and Howard will walk through the door together at 10:15. The team has met twice before to rehearse the intervention and finalize their lists.

Promptly at 10:15, Ed looks up to see Caroline, Melanie, Tom, and Howard enter Bob's office.

Ed: "What's going on?"

Bob: "I'll tell you in a minute, Ed. Caroline, come on in and help the others get situated. Melanie and Tom, it's nice to see you again."

Ed: "I'd think it was my birthday, except that everyone has such a long face. Come on, someone, clear up the mystery."

The team members are seated and ready to begin. As chairperson, Bob begins.

Bob: "Ed, I want you to know that this is going to be tough for all of us. I did want to talk about the report, but the more important reason for this meeting is the one that brought your family here. I'm relieved that we can finally bring it out into the open. None of us had any desire to withhold anything from you, and in fact we were uncomfortable doing so. But we wanted to be sure to do this right.

"Now I'm going to ask you to do something for us, and that's to give us a chance to talk. Promise to listen, however difficult that may be. We know it's not going to be easy for you ... Would you help us by just listening?"

Ed: "What's this all about?"

Bob: "We've been getting together over the past few weeks because we all care about you and are deeply concerned about what's been happening to you. If you'll hear us out, I'm sure you'll understand why we feel as we do. We're here to talk about your drinking, and all we ask is that you hear us out. Will you do that?"

Ed (glaring): "I can't believe this. I thought you wanted me here to work on that report."

Bob: "We're going to table that for right now, because this is really more important."

Ed (turning to face Caroline): "I suppose you're behind this. You've been after me for years about my drinking."

Caroline: "We're all here together because we all care about you, Ed. Melanie and Tom and Bob and Howard and I all care about you very much."

Bob: "Ed, this is really quite serious. I understand that you might be feeling angry right now, but if you decide not to participate, or to keep interrupting, then there could be serious consequences."

Ed: "Are you telling me that my job is at stake?"

Bob (nodding): "It could come to that. But I don't want to talk about that now. Instead, let's all listen to what Melanie has to say."

Ed: "All right, I'll listen. I won't promise to like it, but I'll listen."

Bob: "That's all we ask. Go ahead, Melanie."

Melanie reaches into her purse and takes out her list. She looks nervously at her father before beginning.

Melanie: "Dad, you know that I've always loved you. Nobody could have had a better or more considerate father. I remember all the time we spent together when I was little — especially the camping trip you arranged for the two of us when I was nine.

"But lately I've been really worried about you. Whenever Mom invites me over for dinner, you never make it through the meal without several drinks. And then it seems we always get in an argument. Last Sunday you almost threw a glass at me. That's not like you, Dad. You never raised a hand to me before you started drinking."

Ed: "Melanie, I was just kidding . . ."

Melanie: "I was frightened. Remember I left early? That was why."

Ed: "Well, if that's all . . . ."

Melanie: "It isn't. Last month I brought Sam, a new guy I was dating, over to meet you and Mom. It was obvious that you had already been drinking, but you got out the liquor and started mixing cocktails anyway. Before long you were stumbling around and slurring your words. I was very embarrassed, Dad. And after that I didn't hear from Sam again."

Ed: "Surely you don't think that's my fault!"

Melanie: "Then there was last Christmas eve. I was singing a solo in the church choir, and you and Mom were supposed to come to hear me. She showed up by herself and said that you had the flu. The truth was, you were passed out on the couch. You'd been drinking since early afternoon."

And so it goes, item after item. By the time Melanie has finished reading, Ed is sitting in stony silence. Then Howard begins.

Howard: "Ed, you're the best bridge partner I've ever had. And you've been a good friend for years. But I'm concerned about your drinking, too."

Ed (sarcastically): "Well, Howard, we've tipped a few together, as I recall. Besides, weren't you the one who taught me how to mix the perfect martini?"

Howard: "Ed, the last time we got together for a game you arrived intoxicated. It was obvious to everyone there. Then you proceeded to fix yourself another few drinks over the next hour or so. You couldn't concentrate on the game, and you started telling some long involved story that went nowhere. You played out of turn and finally we had to call it quits."

Ed: "Okay, so I got distracted. There's been a lot on my mind lately."

Howard: "Two weeks ago, when you asked to borrow my car because yours was at the station being serviced, I had to say no. That's because the last time I let you have it, you left it in a parking lot downtown overnight. And you didn't even remember *which* parking lot. Caroline told me that you came home in a cab and that you had been drinking."

Ed: "I found your car the next day, didn't I? Besides, I thought Caroline and I agreed to keep that between the two of us. So much for secrets!"

Howard: "Remember the last time you were invited to Stan's for a party? You not only threw a pass at Elizabeth, you were rude to my wife, too. She decided to brush it off, but she was really upset.

"I had seen you making yourself a drink earlier. You poured a whole glass of bourbon and drank it, and then you mixed yourself another. I know you didn't see me watching. I'm really concerned about you."

Ed: "Great. Now people are spying on me. Are we almost through here?"

Bob: "Ed, please hear us out. We know it isn't easy. It's tough on all of us."

Ed folds his hands across his chest and stares at the ceiling. He is still staring at the ceiling when Howard finishes reading and the turn passes to Tom.

Tom: "Dad, this is hard for me. I'm afraid that you're going to get mad at me. We've already had our share of problems. But I love you, Dad. And I can't sit back and watch you do this to yourself and Mom and me and Melanie."

He takes a deep breath before beginning to read.

Tom: "Dad, remember last summer when we took that camping trip? You kept getting out of the car, supposedly to check the trunk and find out what was rolling around in it. I knew that it was a bottle, and that every time you stopped you were sneaking a drink. By the time we got to the campsite, you were loaded."

Ed: "Tom, that's not fair. I thought we had a great time."

Tom: "Well, we didn't. At least, I didn't. I spent the whole weekend worrying if you were going to stumble into the campfire or get lost in the woods. You were drunk most of the time, Dad. I couldn't wait to get back home."

Ed: "You just wanted to be back here with your friends. I know it's hard for a teenager to spend a weekend with his old man."

Tom: "That's not true! But Dad, it's not any fun when you're drinking. Can't you see what your drinking is doing to all of us? Melanie and Mom and me?"

Bob: "Tom, please keep reading from your list. What's next on your list, Tom?"

Tom is visibly upset. In a moment, he takes another deep breath and starts reading again.

Tom: "Okay. Here goes. A couple of weeks ago I came home late and brought two friends into the house. I admit we made too much noise. Anyway, the next thing I knew you were standing in the kitchen in your pajamas. And you were shouting at me, and swearing at me, in front of my friends. Everyone could tell you were drunk. You were drunk in front of my friends!"

As Tom goes on reading, Ed pretends not to listen. He shifts in his chair, looks at his watch, reties his shoelaces. He avoids the eyes of everyone in the room.

When Tom finishes, Bob pulls his list from his pocket. He lays it on the table in front of him and starts to read from it.

Bob: "Ed, you've always been a terrific employee. During the first five years you were here, sales soared and you were largely responsible. But that's not the case anymore. For the past several months your performance has gone way down."

Ed: "Bob, be realistic. Our whole industry is in trouble."

Bob: "Perhaps, but the only department in our company that's in trouble is yours. Your coworkers are complaining that you're not carrying your share of the workload. Your reports aren't up to snuff. When we lost the Martin account, and I asked Stu Martin why, he told me that he couldn't work with you anymore. He didn't want to say anything against you, but I have suspected for a long time that that account was in trouble because of your drinking."

Ed: "Did he also tell you how much grief he gave me when I was only a week late with his order?"

Bob: "Last Monday you came in from a two-hour lunch reeking of alcohol. You refused to take calls for the rest of the afternoon."

Ed: "I've seen you have a drink during lunch yourself."

Bob: "I don't do it every day. You do. Even when you eat in the cafeteria, you somehow manage to smell of liquor by the middle of the afternoon."

Ed stands up.

Ed: "All right. Wait here. I'll show you."

He leaves the room, and in less than a minute he's back — carrying a bottle. He puts it down in front of Bob.

Ed: "I'll admit, I had it in my desk. Maybe I have an occasional pick-me-up during the day. But that's all over. I'll never do it again, I promise."

Bob: "That's great, Ed, and I'm sure you mean it: But the rest of the group and I have decided that you need help sticking to that kind of decision."

Ed: "What do you mean, help? Are you talking about detox or something?"

Bob: "Let's listen to what Caroline has to say, and then we'll let you decide. Ready, Caroline?"

Caroline stares down at her list as if trying to memorize it. Everyone waits quietly. Finally she looks up and at her husband.

Caroline: "Ed, I married you because I loved you, and I still love you. But I'm at the end of my rope. Lately I've been tempted to ask you to move out, to leave Tom and me alone. I'm scared when you drink, and I'm afraid that you might hurt us.

"Two weeks ago you didn't get home from work until 10:00. When I asked you where you'd been, you hit me and told me to mind my own business. In all the years we've been together, nothing like that has ever happened."

Tom (shocked): "Mom! You never said anything about that in our other meetings."

Caroline: "I wanted to say it to your father first. I wanted to let him know that for the first time in more than 25 years of marriage, he frightens me."

Ed looks down from the ceiling at Caroline, and some of the defensiveness goes out of his posture.

Ed: "Honey, I'm really sorry. I don't know what got into me. I swear it will never happen again."

Caroline: "I just want you to get better, so things can be the way they used to be. Ed, I've been handling the checkbook for months now. I've been covering your bad checks, and sorting out your financial messes, and taking money out of our savings to make up for the overdrafts. Last month you overdrew more than $500 and never even realized it. The more you drink, the more the money seems to disappear. You used to keep track of every penny you spent."

Ed: "I make a good salary. I don't have to keep track of every penny anymore. We have plenty to live on."

Caroline: "Last month you left your wallet in a bar. You didn't even notice until three days later. I was on the phone immediately to department stores and bank card companies, but whoever took your wallet had three whole days to use your cards. I told our creditors some made-up story about where you'd lost it because I was ashamed to tell the truth."

Ed squirms in his chair. Caroline continues reading.

Caroline: "Last week, when we went out to dinner, I had to sneak the car keys out of your jacket and hide them in my purse so you wouldn't insist on driving. You had finished off a bottle and a half of wine all by yourself. I wasn't about to get in the passenger seat."

Ed: "I'm a safe driver. Have I ever had an accident?"

Caroline (speaking very softly): "Not yet. But three weeks ago you came awfully close. Remember when that little boy ran out from between the parked cars? I had to grab the wheel. You'd been drinking that afternoon — even though you hid the bottle in the garage, I knew you'd been drinking — and if I hadn't reacted as quickly as I had, you would have hit that little boy. And you might have killed him."

For the first time, Ed has nothing to say.

Caroline: "I'm not going to cover for you anymore. I'm not going to tell people like Melanie that you have the flu when you're really sleeping off a drunk. I'm not going to call Bob and make excuses for your tardiness. And I'm not going to stick around and wait until you really do hurt me or Tom. It has to stop, Ed."

By now Ed is looking down at the floor.

Bob: "We're almost through, Ed. I know this is painful, but we're almost through. Everyone has one or two more things to say to you. When they're finished, we can all talk."

Melanie: "Dad, I hardly know how to say this, but I don't even like coming home anymore. I never know what condition I'm going to find you in. It used to be such a happy house, and now there's so much tension. It makes me want to stay away."

Howard: "Ed, I value your friendship, and I can't stand to see this happening. And I can't have you over to our house anymore until things change. Linda cares about you, too, but she feels protective of the kids. She doesn't want you around them when you've been drinking."

Caroline: "Ed, I can't go on this way any longer. Your drinking is affecting me, too. Sometimes I think I'm going crazy. We don't talk anymore, we don't do things together like we used to, and I feel that I have to watch over you every second. One thing I've learned in these past few weeks is that I'm as sick as you are. We *all* need help, Ed."

Melanie: "Mom is right, Dad. What you've got is a disease called chemical dependency, and it's catching. We've got it, too, Tom and Mom and I, in our own way.

"But you don't have to stay sick, and neither do we. You can get better. You can get better. We can all get better, but we have to stick together."

Tom: "Dad, please say yes. I love you, Dad. We all love you, and we don't like to see you like this. You're not the same person I used to know. I'm ashamed to ask people over to the house because I never know what shape you're going to be in. I feel like I don't have a father anymore."

Bob: "I mean what I said earlier, Ed. You've got to get your performance back up. But I don't think you can until you accept some help for your drinking problem."

Ed covers his face with his hands. After a moment or two, he looks up and into the faces of everyone in the room. When he speaks, it is barely a whisper.

Ed: "Good Lord, is it possible that everything you're saying is true? Have I really been such a jerk?"

Caroline: "We're not here to call you a jerk or to blame you for anything, but to get all of us some help. I know I need it as much as you do."

Ed: "Well, just what is it you want me to do? Do you want me to pack my things and move out? Is that what you want?"

Caroline: "No, it's not what we want. We want you to get better."

Bob: "Ed, alcoholism is a disease. With help, you can get well again."

Ed: "I don't understand. What do you mean, a disease? I can stop drinking whenever I want to. And I will, starting today. You'll see!"

Bob: "The people who will help you can tell you more about the disease. Quitting drinking is a lot harder than you think. Besides, there's more to it than that."

Ed (resolutely): "Bob, you know that when I make up my mind to do something, I do it. I mean what I'm saying: I'll never take another drink in my life."

Bob (looking Ed straight in the eye): "We're not here to have you promise you'll quit again. We're here to have you agree to accept help. It's time to try something new and different."

Ed: "What are you talking about — Alcoholics Anonymous or something like that? Some club for drunks and derelicts?"

Bob: "I think you'd be surprised by the kinds of people who go to A.A. But that's not where we want you to start. You can go to Park City Hospital, or you can go to North Treatment Center. They're expecting you at either place today."

Ed (obviously stunned): "*Today*? Wait just a minute. We have to talk about this some more. Besides, I can't go today. That report is due on Monday."

Bob: "We'll take care of it here. We can manage for a month without you. Besides, when you get back, you'll be so much better that you'll probably be twice as productive."

Ed: "A *month*? Did I hear you say a month?"

Bob: "That's how long the treatment program lasts. You go in today, and you come out 30 days from now."

Ed turns to Caroline.

Ed: "I can't leave you and Tom for a month."

Caroline: "I'll visit as soon as they'll let me. And I'll be there every day during Family Week."

Ed: "But it will take time to get ready and pack, and you probably have to make a reservation or something . . . Can't it wait until Monday?"

Caroline: "Your suitcase is already packed and ready to go. It's in the trunk of my car. If you need any other clothes, I'll make sure you get them."

Bob: "And if you go today, your job will be waiting for you when you return."

Ed: "And if I don't?"

Bob: "That's the only alternative you have, friend. I can't accept any other."

By now Ed is crying softly. Melanie moves to stand behind him and puts her arms around him.

Melanie: "Dad, this is going to help us all. You'll get better, and we'll get better too. Mom and I are going to our first Al-Anon meeting tonight."

Ed: "I can't believe this is happening. Why didn't anybody say anything about this earlier? Why didn't anybody tell me what I was doing to you?"

Caroline: "We all tried, but you didn't believe us. I understand now why that was. You couldn't see how sick you were. You didn't know. It's all right, Ed."

Bob: "Now we've got a decision to make. Which will it be, Ed? Park City or North?"

Early that afternoon, Ed checks into North Treatment Center. His wife and children are there for support. The intervention has been a success: Ed will get the help he needs.

The intervention described above proceeded exactly according to plan. That plan can be summarized by what we call the Five

Principles of Intervention:

1. Meaningful persons in the life of the chemically dependent person are involved.

2. All of the meaningful persons write down specific data about the events and behaviors involving the dependent person's chemical use which legitimatize their concern.

3. All of the meaningful persons tell the dependent person how they feel about what has been happening in their lives, and they do it in a nonjudgmental way.

4. The victim is offered specific choices — *this* treatment center, or *that* hospital.

Had Ed absolutely refused to consider either of these choices and vowed to quit drinking on his own, then the team would have presented the "What-If" question: "What if you do start drinking again? What if you have just one more drink?" They would have made an agreement with Ed that *if* he began using again, he would accept help. And they would have made him stick to it!

5. When the victim agrees to accept help, it is made available immediately.

At the Johnson Institute, we have learned that *if a team sticks to this plan, its chances of succeeding are eight in ten.* In my personal experience, I have expected it to work every time — and it has. A crack appears in the victim's wall of defenses and he or she agrees to accept some form of help.

As you will learn from researching the various treatment options available in your area, there are many available today, ranging from outpatient counseling to full-scale inpatient programs. The latter option merits some brief discussion here.

An inpatient treatment program typically begins with detoxi-fication — safely withdrawing the patient from the toxic effects of alcohol or drugs. The patient is given a thorough medical examination, and other problems are targeted for follow-up care.

The next step is the education of the patient — about himself or herself, and about the disease of chemical dependency. This is accomplished in meetings with counselors, in regular lectures, and in daily encounter sessions with other patients.

The primary purpose of the group sessions is to identify the patient's defenses and describe them in ways that he or she will be able to understand and recognize. These are no-nonsense, confrontive, and sometimes painful times. The wall of defenses doesn't just crack; it breaks down and stays down as a result of the caring interaction of fellow patients and staff.

During these sessions, emphasis is also placed on the patient's *good* qualities. Self-hatred is countered by praise, encourage-ment, and the genuine affection which often forms among group members. The wonderful discovery that "maybe I'm not all bad" forms the foundation for hope and recovery.

At some point during this process, the patient begins to *see* himself or herself — perhaps for the first time. He or she comes to terms with the disease and its stark realities. As one recovering alcoholic said, "I had stopped drinking for periods of time before, because I knew I shouldn't drink. Then, at last, it dawned on me that *I had to stop because I couldn't quit.*" This growing awareness is balanced by the belief that things can and will get better.

The inpatient program is followed by an aftercare program of approximately two years. Patient and spouse attend weekly "growth group" meetings. Progress is tracked and interpersonal relationships are explored.

Another ongoing part of recovery is weekly attendance at A.A. meetings. Spouses go to Al-Anon; teen-age children to Alateen.

The success rates for this kind of treatment are high, ranging anywhere from 50 percent to 80 percent, depending on the program and the motivation of the victim and his or her family. *Intervention is the key to motivation.* In the majority of cases, the disease is arrested and the chemically dependent person undergoes a successful recovery.

What If the Intervention Doesn't Work?

What if the victim doesn't agree to accept help then and there? *Keep trying.* Don't give up! Remember that the victim's life depends on your continuing commitment.

We have found that intervention tends to have a cumulative effect. If the initial session doesn't propel the person into treatment, the second probably will — or the third. Sometimes it takes even more effort on the part of the team members to break down the victim's defense system. Rationalization, projection, denial, repression, and self-delusion combine to create a barrier to self-awareness that rivals the Great Wall of China.

But what of the truly "incorrigible" drinker, or the one who walks out of the intervention and never comes back, or the one who really is "too far gone" for help? If that person continues drinking and never enters treatment, has the intervention been a failure?

No, it has not. *Properly done*, intervention works every time. *Properly done*, there are no failures. Here are the reasons why:

- The people who do the intervening — the team members — are forever changed. They know that they are not alone. They know that help and support are available to them. Their lives are never the same afterward.
- The family unit is also changed — from the immobilized, fearful, guilty, shame-ridden group they once were to an

entirely new dynamic. They know what chemical dependency is. They see its symptoms *in themselves*, and they seek help *for themselves*. They come to see that the chemically dependent person's sickness is *not their fault*. What a liberating realization this is!

- Finally, the victim is changed in relation to the drug. The crack in the wall of defenses has admitted knowledge that he or she will never again be able to fully deny. (As one spouse remarked, "At least we spoiled his drinking!")

In sum, intervention always has *some* effect, and that effect is invariably positive. There is no way it can ever make things worse. At the very least, it offers a chance for recovery where before none existed; at the most, it starts the whole family on the path toward fully living again.

It is to be hoped that these observations will move you to try yet one more time, if your first intervention does not result in the victim immediately accepting treatment.

Getting Help for Yourself

It is wise to seek help for yourself regardless of the outcome of the intervention. Part I of this book describes the many ways in which the people around the alcoholic — especially family members — are trapped by the dynamics of the disease. Chemical dependency is contagious, and there is certainly no stigma involved in getting assistance with your own recovery.

Before we go any further, let us dispel a few misconceptions about family therapy.

- First, the family does not undergo treatment for the sake of the chemically dependent person.
- Second, the sobriety of the chemically dependent person does not depend on the rehabilitation of the chemically dependent

family. (The person's disease is not your fault; neither is his or her recovery your responsibility.)

- And third, family recovery does not depend on the future sobriety of the chemically dependent person.

When talking about family recovery, the point at issue is this: Because chemical dependency develops into a family illness, virtually *all* family members need some kind of help in recovery. Furthermore, if the chemical dependency has existed in the family over a long period of time, it is most likely that *all* family members will need some kind of outside help in restoring themselves to a state of health and happiness.

For the family, this usually means a program of family care, individual counseling, and regular, active involvement in Al-Anon, Alateen, or an Adult Children of Alcoholics group.

Why does the family need a program for recovery? Most families are so close to the problem of chemical dependency that their recognition of its scope is dulled and severely limited. In their efforts to protect themselves from the pain and ravages of the disease, they have developed their own restricted and emotionally insufficient ways of coping, and they have stumbled into an emotionally crippled life. Although their problems may have originated around someone else's chemical use, they will not necessarily go away even if that person sobers up.

The best known and most readily accessible method of family care is active participation in Al-Anon and its junior counterpart, Alateen. These two organizations were founded to provide group support and a program for living. The program is almost identical to that of A.A., and both organizations operate on similar principles of confidentiality and self-help. You may find local chapters of Al-Anon and Alateen by consulting your telephone directory.

Many people have also found help and relief from the services of *psychotherapy*. However, these are usually expensive and therefore not always available.

Yet another option is a *family care treatment program*. Such a program provides personal counseling for all family members, as well as mutually supportive group sessions at which they can talk about their problems with other persons who are experiencing the same kinds of troubles.

Family treatment programs also provide accurate information about the disease of chemical dependency, how it affects both the victim and those around him or her, and what methods have worked for other people in recovery. If necessary, referrals are made to additional sources of help.

Because they work with families over long periods of time, family care treatment programs can also help people to test and learn new behaviors for coping with their problems and fulfilling their needs. Find out about the ones in your area by contacting the resources listed on page 74.

For family members, just as for the chemically dependent person, recovery means breaking through the wall of defenses and letting in reality. Like the chemically dependent person, they must learn that alcohol and/or drugs are the focus of the problem, and they must realize that each person in a chemically dependent family is responsible for his or her own behavior, feelings, and recovery. They must become aware that they have choices, that enabling did not and will not help the chemically dependent person to stop using, and that enabling cannot help them to meet their own emotional needs.

Most persons who have been raised in chemically dependent families have never developed the ability to experience a full range of feelings. Recovering the rich and rewarding feeling of life that is part and parcel of the healthy family system may take time to accomplish. But whatever time it takes, it is worth the effort.

What if the chemically dependent person continues to resist all of your efforts to help him or her? Don't allow this to block your own recovery. In fact, a new and vibrant glow on the faces of family members may have the effect of putting even more pressure on the already overburdened victim. Your good health will make his or her drinking or drug use even more uncomfortable. He or she will feel even more left out. And that may cause the breach in the wall you may never have expected to see.

EPILOGUE

Intervention with chemically dependent individuals is an important step in the direction of treating one of the most widespread diseases in our culture. In the face of the statistics, however — the millions of people who are directly affected, and the millions of others who are raised in unhealthy family systems — that step seems pitifully insufficient.

If humankind is ever to truly conquer the disease of chemical dependency, as it has conquered the equally horrible afflictions of polio and smallpox, we must intervene with our society at large, a society that actively promotes the use of alcohol and drugs. We must begin by spreading the word that chemical dependency is in fact a disease, and not a sign of moral weakness or the lack of willpower.

The tragedy of our current society is that so few people understand what chemical dependency is and how it functions. Families remain locked in ignorance over generations. *But there are miracles at work in the world.* Every day someone, somewhere encounters a glimmer of expectation that something can be done. And that person becomes the entrance into the closed family system.

Over the years, the people at the Johnson Institute have heard countless parents and spouses and children say, "My father (or mother, or brother, or sister, or friend, or employee) is an alcoholic. We all knew it, but we believed that nothing could be done. Then one day I happened to pick up a pamphlet that said something about 'intervention' — Does it work? Can I do it? Can it make the person well again?" And we joyfully respond *yes* to all three questions.

We do not yet have the manpower in the professional world to address the problem in its entirety. There are thousands of us —but there are at least 20 million chemically dependent people! Thankfully, there are twice as many, four times as many, even ten times as many concerned persons. And untold numbers of these have taken some successful action.

As you go out and try to help the chemically dependent person in your life, please be assured of my prayers.

Vernon Johnson

1986

Index

Call Johnson Institute TOLL-FREE:
In U.S.: 1-800-231-5165
In Canada: 1-800-447-6660
In Minnesota: 1-800-247-0484

Johnson Institute
7205 Ohms Lane
Minneapolis, MN 55439-2159
(612) 831-1630

Need a copy for a friend?
You may order directly.

INTERVENTION:
HOW TO HELP SOMEONE WHO DOESN'T WANT HELP
A step-by-step guide for families and friends
of chemically dependent persons

by Vernon Johnson
founder and president emeritus of The Johnson Institute
and author of the classic *I'll Quit Tomorrow*

$8.95

Order Form

Please send _____ copy (copies) of INTERVENTION: HOW TO HELP
SOMEONE WHO DOESN'T WANT HELP by Vernon Johnson.

Price $8.95 per copy. Please add $1.50 shipping for the first book and 25¢ for
each additional copy.

_____

Name (please print)

_____

Address

_____

City/State/Zip

_____ ( )_____

Attention   *Telephone*

Please note that orders under $75.00 must be pre-paid.

If paying by credit card, please complete the   For faster service, call our
following: Order Department TOLL FREE:
☐ Bill the full payment to my credit card.   **1-800-231-5165**
☐ VISA ☐ MasterCard ☐ American Express   In Minnesota call:
                                          1-800-247-0484

Credit card number: _____

For MASTERCARD: In Canada call:
                                          1-800-447-6660

Write the 4 digits below the account number: _____

Expiration date: _____ Signature on card: _____

Return this order form to: The Johnson Institute
                             7205 Ohms Lane
                             Minneapolis, MN 55439-2159

Ship to (if different from above):

Name _____

Address _____

City/State/Zip _____